waiting
TO GO HOME

letters and reminiscences
from the Evacuation 1939-45

Martin L Parsons

First Published 1999
by DSM
The Studio
Denton
Peterborough
Cambs PE7 3SD

A catalogue record of this book is available from the British Library

ISBN 0 9536516 0 6

Produced by
DSM
The Studio
Denton
Peterborough
Cambs PE7 3SD

Design and Layout by Marc Lowen
Cartoons by Mic Lowen

Printed in England by Page Bros. Norwich

Publishers' Acknowledgements

The publishers would like to thank all those who have contributed material for this book. The task of selecting what to include has not been easy and the space could have been filled many times over.

Every effort has been made to find the owners of the copyright of all the material used in the book and we apologise to any that may have been missed.

Due to the ravages of time many of the original documents and photographs in the book are of poor quality and where possible we have done our best to improve the quality during reproduction.

Picture Credits

Dorset Record Office, Dorchester
Pages 13, 19, 20, 47, 53, 147, 148

Hampshire Record Office, Winchester
Page 21

The Great Western Railway - a New History. Frank Booker 1977
Pages 33, 34

Devon Record Office, Exeter
Page 54

Imperial War Museum
Page 74

Wiltshire Records Office, Trowbridge
Page 101

Personal Collections

Gordon Brooks Pages 50, 51

Doug Dielhenn Pages 67-68

John Gould Pages 70, 72

Len Davies Pages 77-79

Brian Balding Pages 80, 81

Norma Campin Page 120

Patricia Johnston Pages 150-165

Charles Springitt Page 167

Contents

introduction

It was difficult to decide how best to use these resources, but in the end I decided to use the testimony in both a chronological and thematic way telling the story from 1939-45.

Contributors are referred to by their initials and not by name as some wished to remain anonymous. However, in some instances, I have indicated where they were evacuated from and their eventual destination. Some readers may recognise place names, schools or events, therefore, should they wish to do so, they can contact me via the publishers, and I may be able to put them in contact with the correspondents.

Wherever possible I have transcribed the letters, or parts of letters, verbatim but, because some hand-written letters have been difficult to read, I apologise for any mistakes in the spelling of place names.

If you were an evacuee and having read the accounts here, are moved to write down your reminiscences, please send them to me via the publishers. Your memories, along with many others, will be housed in the Evacuee Resource Centre at the University of Reading library, Bulmershe Court.

Martin L. Parsons 1999

THE beginning

This first letter provides an indication of how the pre-war experiences of some evacuees were so narrow and, in consequence, how much of a wrench and how great an undertaking evacuation actually was. In the 1990s, with the world getting ever smaller in terms of communications and travel, it is worth remembering that for some children in the 1930s and 40s their whole life experience was limited to a very small physical environment.

'We were living in West Ham in those days, our world a very small one, encompassed by a few streets. We went to Forest Gate to school and that made us different and we didn't know the local children as well as we would have done had we gone to school with them. School, church and Forest Gate were one thing, quite normal but in a compartment by itself. To wander into other areas, for instance by Plaistow station, was really like going into foreign parts. We didn't belong there and felt adventurous just being there. Even going on to the 'Sewer Bank' just at the bottom of our road, was something very daring, and as for 'The Cut' over the back, that was forbidden, although we sneaked there on more than one occasion.

On summer evenings we played in the street and enjoyed being included in the games, especially skipping. I remember vividly everyone coming out to skip, the little ones, the big ones, those who had just left school and best of all...the Mums. We had a huge rope, right across the road and we played all kinds of games. I loved to see the Mums 'jumping in' when they were called and the excitement of 'all ee in together girls' with a whole crowd crammed in skipping together.

As children we were aware of the threat of war in the air, especially after Munich, and I remember getting very frightened. We had heard a lot about the First World War from our parents and grandparents, and, although I had always thought it rather dull and often wished they would talk of something else, enough of what they had said sunk in and caused me to be very fearful'.

K.G. Cambridge

'In September 1939, after War was declared, everyone was anxious 'to do something to help'. Nothing appeared to be happening, except that Air Raid Precautions were obvious, men were being called up. There was the blackout and Petrol rationing etc. My friends and I, as keen members of the School's Boy Scout Troop (11th Exeter. Hele's School), got together and offered our services, which clearly were not required. All they could find us to do was to clear space in drawers and cupboards by destroying papers at the local hospital'.

A.S.D.

THE
planning

C. P. BRUTTON,
CLERK OF THE PEACE
AND
ERK OF THE COUNTY COUNCIL
OF DORSET.
TELEPHONE & TELEGRAMS:
DORCHESTER 500.

OFFICIAL COMMUNICATIONS SHOULD
BE ADDRESSED IMPERSONALLY TO
"THE CLERK OF THE PEACE" OR TO
"THE CLERK OF THE COUNTY COUNCIL".

COUNTY OFFICES,

DORCHESTER, DORSET.

30th September, 1938.

Dear Sir,

I am informed by the Home Office that they have authorised the evacuation of 30,000 children from the Borough of Croydon to Dorsetshire and I am requested, in consultation with the Clerks to Rural and Urban Districts in the County, to make arrangements as soon as possible for the accommodation of this number of refugees.

I shall therefore be glad if you will let me have the names and addresses of persons to be appointed as billeting officers (which should be about 1 officer for every 100 refugees) for your area when I will issue to them a form of authority to act.

I enclose a copy of instructions to billeting officers for your information and assistance and will also forward a copy to each billeting officer with his authority.

I also enclose a list of the Croydon Secondary and Elementary school children which you would be expected to accommodate in your area and shall be glad if you would instruct the billeting officers to make provisional arrangements for billets immediately pending the receipt of their official authority.

Yours faithfully,

C. P. R.

Clerk of the County Council.

P.S. It is anticipated that all necessary expenditure will be met out of National Funds and I shall therefore be obliged if you will keep a separate account.

To. The Clerks to the Borough, Urban and Rural District Councils in the County of Dorset.

Note the date. This letter, from the Clerk of the Dorset County Council to Clerks of the Boroughs, Urban and Rural District Councils, was prompted by the Government's plan to evacuate children from London during the Munich Crisis.

The following two accounts are rare in as much as they are from the Host and the female evacuee who stayed with her in 1939.

The Host

'Memories of August 1939.

We had moved from London in March 1938 to a pretty Berkshire village, Waltham St. Lawrence. Hitler had taken over the Sudetenland that year and there were rumours of war. But life went on and it was not until August 1939 when we lost all hope of 'Peace in our time!'

At this point we were all asked to attend a meeting in the Village Hall. We were told that arrangements were being made to evacuate children and young mothers from all the cities and big towns and that we would have London children. We were to expect streams of people-'Shadow Trekkers'- I remember they called them, and we should be ready to house them and give them sustenance. Someone had a vivid imagination and had obviously seen pictures of Russian refugees plodding along dreary roads with all their possessions on a hand cart and falling by the wayside from exhaustion. So there were tins of biscuits, tea, dried milk and First Aid kits stored in the Village Hall in anticipation.

We were told how many children each home was to accommodate. We then waited for the day to come when we would be called upon to help these unfortunate 'Shadow Trekkers'.

In point of fact they arrived in coaches from East Ham in a very orderly fashion - no sore feet or bundles of belongings. They had their names written on labels pinned on to their coats and each carried a gas mask and a small suitcase. Some of them looked sad and bewildered, others excited and curious.

They were given tea and biscuits and then told where they were to stay. We got into our cars and ferried them to their new 'homes'. We were to have a 14 year old, Mary and her 5 year old brother 'Tiddler', we never did know his real name! When I went over to fetch them I saw Mary was trying to cut a piece of soap in half. I asked her why she was doing this and she said that her sister was going somewhere else and they only had one piece of soap. I could not see a family divided so I said Dolly could come with us also. She was ten.

Thus started our education into how the other half lived.

The whole proceedings had gone very smoothly and certainly our village coped well with the influx'.

N.H-S. Kew

The Evacuee

'Dolly to her host. (Written in 1996).

I remember arriving in the village of Waltham St. Lawrence with my three brothers and sister Mary. We all wore identification labels. I don't recall being frightened just interested in the activity around. You were one of the car owners and were carrying a clipboard with a list of names and addresses. We all got into your car and after a short drive you stopped, looked at the board and said 'Yes, Mrs H.... wants two boys about 9 years'. We drove to Mrs H... house. She came down the path, a very stern looking tall woman and took my brother Billy and my stepbrother Ken inside. When I saw them at school later they had their heads completely shaved. I expect they were lousy as we all were.

We drove on a little further and you suddenly looked in the mirror and said 'How would you like to come and live with me?' I was pleased as you looked so lovely. We drove down the long drive and the door was opened by a maid in uniform. As we went in I tripped on the step and fell into the hall. Instead of the expected clip around the ear for being clumsy, you and Mona, the maid, were full of concern. This started the only happy memories of childhood and I have treasured them and thought about you with love and gratitude throughout my life. I remember you always bathed Tiddler and me yourself although you had two maids. We were bathed and put to bed and you read to us until the dinner gong went.

We had a delightful bedroom very clean and comfortable a complete contrast to our home where we slept 'top to tail', 6 in a bed with no sheets and pillow cases. At home the place was infested with bugs and we had paraffin sprayed on to the walls each night, no windows open; you can imagine the smell.

I have many happy memories of playing in the woods near the house, the local hunt (the Garth), scrumping apples from the austere looking house up the lane, in fact not scrumping but openly taking your gardener's wheelbarrow and stripping a whole tree. I came back triumphant to Sallie the cook and presented them to her. I remember when we threw porridge out of the nursery window onto the nectarines and when Albert, the gardener, complained you didn't punish us but set up a little plot of our own. You bought us Wellington boots and a fork and trowel and we spent happy times digging in our own garden.

When Christmas came we had toys for the first time ever. We were surrounded by love and happiness.

When we heard we were leaving I remember going down the lane and lying in a field of cowslips and crying. Apart from a few months spent in children's home where life was quite pleasant, my time with you and your family was like a wonderland and a happy release from a very traumatic and unhappy childhood.

You said you thought we went back to London, but in fact I went to another couple. My stepmother told me years later that she had asked for me to be moved as we were too comfortable.

Later I went into a children's home in Maidenhead. I went back to London when I was 13 as my stepmother had had a baby and I was needed to queue for food etc. When the Blitz started in earnest my father, stepmother and baby went into the country and left me there alone, having turned off the water and electricity. I wasn't afraid, just glad to be free and I just went into the Anderson shelter when the sirens went and to a neighbours house to wash.

I left at 16 and went to Cornwall to work in a children's home. I didn't see my brothers and sisters again.

Dolly'.

EVACUATION TEST ORDERS FOR CHILDREN

READY FOR MONDAY'S REHEARSALS

Thousands of children in the evacuation areas of England and Scotland today had their first experience of a Saturday at school.

All over London and in every town in the evacuation schedule teachers and pupils answered the Ministry of Health's appeal for them to go back to school. In many cases teachers had hurried back from their holidays. At every secondary and elementary school in the listed areas they waited for their classes to take their places as on a normal "term" day.

CAREFUL INSTRUCTIONS

Quietly and without any fuss, the children were told why they had been sent for, and were given careful instructions about the full dress evacuation rehearsal which the Ministry has asked to be carried out on Monday. The children were told to report to their schools with gas-masks.

Having received their instructions, they spent the remainder of the day at their lessons.

Dorset Daily Echo
26th August 1939

'I was evacuated at the end of August 1939 from the City of Portsmouth. On two occasions, during the early part of August, we had been told to report to the school, bringing a haversack with a change of clothes, toilet accessories and of course our gas-mask, sandwiches and a drink. On both of these occasions we had thought it great fun, as we would walk around the playground in twos and then through the gate where our Mothers were waiting to take us home to eat our sandwiches!

However, at the end of August we went quite happily into school and everything was the same, only this time there were buses waiting and we were told to climb aboard and were whisked away to the railway station where a train was waiting. There were no goodbyes to our mothers'.

M.H. Bristol

'In 1939 I was a pupil in the Prep. department of Chatham County School. Schooldays progressed normally throughout the year until the end of August holiday when we, who were to be evacuated, attended school for informal lessons and to practise the procedure for evacuation. This included instructions on the amount of luggage we could take (I carried a large rucksack because this was as much as I could manage), suitable clothing to wear, including the obligatory gas mask, a packet of sandwiches, and of course my beloved teddy-bear (*)...

At last the day came. It was Friday 1st September that our mothers had to take up to the school where we said our goodbyes, formed a long crocodile of 198 children from my school together with 65 brothers and sisters from other schools and teachers and marched to Chatham Station with the leaders carrying a banner, presumably showing the name of the school. It was an extremely hot September day. We felt the heat more probably because we were wearing our winter gym slips, Macs, and velour hats for the coming of winter'.

M.H-J. Glamorgan

(*) This evacuee was lucky because many Evacuating Authorities did not allow children to take teddy-bears, dolls or other toys because they would take up too much space. Although, you will read later that one correspondent was allowed to take his stamp album with him. No such restrictions were placed on those children evacuated privately.

'During the summer of 1939 we had a caravan holiday at Lymchurch in Kent. Upon our return I recall the preparations for War. The cigarette cards we collected and swapped, had Air Raid Precaution details, one depicted large balloons floating over the houses, linked to each other by cables. It was still the school summer holidays. Peckham Fire Station was where we boys held open the sacks the men filled with sand. Most of the doors and windows of the station were sandbagged against bomb blast.

'You are going to the country for safety', we were told. It will be a holiday. It had been decided that my younger brother James and I would be evacuated with my sister's school, Peckham Central School for girls. Our second brother was to go with his own school, Peckham Central School for Boys. Our older brother was at work. Sad to relate that this was the very last time our happy family were all together...the war took its toll.

We attended our sister's school for a whole week. Each day we said our farewells and left home with a fibre suitcase containing some clothes, sandwiches and the one toy we were allowed, mine was a cigarette card album. During the week linen covers were made for our gas mask boxes by the girls. We boys had our own special classes, but we all practised parading and marching around the school grounds.

Monday through to Thursday we went back home each afternoon and ate our sandwiches for tea. On the Friday as we once again went to school, we noticed all the plane trees along the main road had been painted with three white bands to aid visibility in the black out. Outside Oliver Goldsmiths School, double decker buses were waiting. To recall one's exact feelings at the time after so many years is not possible, probably excitement, for that was my nature as a child'.

J.R. Dartford

INFORMATION ON

EVACUATION

FOR HOUSEHOLDERS

taking

UNACCOMPANIED CHILDREN

Issued by THE WOMEN'S VOLUNTARY SERVICES for CIVIL DEFENCE

SPECIMEN MEALS SUITABLE FOR A CHILD OF SCHOOL AGE

BREAKFAST.	DINNER.	TEA. (With an apple and perhaps bread and butter* before going to bed
1. Weak tea or milk / Porridge or other cereal, milk and sugar / Bread and dripping or butter*	Roast beef or mutton / Potatoes / Greens / Currant Roll.	Weak tea or milk / Bread and butter* / Cheese / Jam.
2. Weak tea or milk / Cold ham / Bread and butter*	Lentil Soup or / Minced meat and tomatoes / Potatoes / Jam Tart.	Weak tea or milk / Bread and butter* / Lettuce or watercress.
3. Weak tea or milk / Fried bacon / Bread and butter*	Stewed steak and onions / Potatoes / Carrots / Baked bread pudding.	Cocoa or milk / Bread and butter* / Jam.
4. Weak tea or milk / Porridge, milk and sugar / Bread and butter* / Jam.	Steak pudding / Potatoes / Greens / Raw fruit (orange or apple)	Weak tea or milk / Potted meat / Bread and butter*
5. Weak tea or milk / Fried potatoes / Bread and jam.	Boiled Silverside / Potatoes / Carrots / Milk pudding.	Weak tea or milk / Cheese / Bread and butter* / Dates.
6. Weak tea or milk / Egg / Bread and butter*	Steak Pie / Potatoes / Beans or peas / Raw fruit (orange or apple).	Cocoa or milk / Bread and butter* / Jam.
7. Weak tea or milk / Porridge, milk and sugar / Bread and butter* or dripping	Hot-pot / Boiled apricot pudding	Weak tea or milk / Cheese / Bread and butter*
8. Weak tea or milk / Herrings / Bread and butter*	Meat and vegetable pie / Potatoes / Stewed fruit and custard.	Cocoa or milk / Bread and butter* / Watercress or lettuce / Cake.
9. Weak tea or milk / Porridge or other cereal, milk and sugar / Bread and butter* or dripping	Fish Pie or Fish Cakes / Pickled beetroot / Boiled apple pudding.	Cocoa or milk / Potted meat / Salad / Bread and butter*
10. Cocoa or milk / Finnan haddock / Bread and butter*	Stewed Liver and onions / or / Stewed rabbit or mutton / Potatoes, Greens / Milk pudding.	Weak tea or milk / Baked beans and tomatoes / Bread and butter*

*—Or margarine.

This leaflet, designed to help hosts plan meals for evacuees and to provide basic details about the evacuation, was issued by the WVS at the time the scheme was implemented. It is obvious from the 'Simple Rules ...' section, that they were expecting many householders not to know anything about child care!!

1. RESPONSIBILITY

When you receive unaccompanied children into your home you will be expected to control and care for them as if they were your own. If any difficulty should arise consult your Local Authority, i.e., the Clerk to the local Council or whoever has been appointed to act for him in your town or village.

2. PAYMENT

You will receive 10s. 6d. a week for one child or 8s. 6d. a week for each child if you are taking more than one. This covers full board and lodging, but not clothes or medical expenses.

You will be given a form by the billeting officer which can be cashed at the local Post Office. Payment will be made weekly in advance.

3. RATIONS

The children and those with them will have received emergency rations to cover the first 48 hours, and it is hoped that there will not be a rush on the shops, where only minor purchases should be made during that period.

4. BEDDING and CLOTHES

Children will not bring any bedding with them. If you need extra tell your local authority. The children will have hand luggage with a change of clothes. When the clothes, boots or shoes need repairing or replacing, if the parents have not sent further supplies, you should report to the local authority.

5. ILLNESS

If any of the children billeted with you become ill send for the local Doctor or District Nurse in the ordinary way. They will have extra staff for this purpose and you will not be expected to pay.

6. EDUCATION

Arrangements will be made for the children to continue their education, and in consequence the schools may have to work in shifts.

7. COMMUNAL MEALS

In many districts it may be possible to arrange for the children to have their mid-day meal at a communal centre. If the children in your charge have meals there you will have to pay a small sum out of the allowances you receive.

SIMPLE RULES FOR THE CARE OF CHILDREN

In order to keep a child healthy and happy the diet must be well balanced with plenty of variety.

Children should be fed at regular hours, the heaviest meal being in the middle of the day, and the last meal should preferably be at least one hour before bed-time ; three meals a day is generally considered best.

If possible a child should have a pint of milk daily, a certain amount of which may be included in the cooking.

Children should be given plenty of water to drink. Also fresh green vegetables, tomatoes and fruits (especially oranges) to eat whenever possible.

They should not be allowed to take violent exercise or bathe immediately after a meal.

Baths should be given as often as possible, but at least once a week. It would be better to have a tin basin of fresh water for each child than to allow them to share a bath.

Each child's face flannel, towel, toothbrush, brush and comb and other personal belongings should be marked and kept separate.

Bedroom windows should be kept open at night and it should be remembered that young children need 11 hours' sleep.

Make sure you have some bandages and lint for minor accidents and the District Nurse will advise you on what remedies to keep in the house.

If you can spare the time to do so, you are strongly recommended to attend any simple Home Nursing or Child Welfare Lectures that may be available.

Do not forget that the children will be in strange surroundings and may be homesick. You should watch them carefully.

FOOD STORAGE AND MENUS

In drawing up Menus remember that the following foodstuffs would be rationed in War Time:—Butcher's Meats, Cooking Fats (including lard and dripping), Bacon and Ham, Sugar, Butter and Margarine.

Householders are recommended to buy and store now an additional week's requirements of certain foods. The number of children expected should be borne in mind when calculating the week's requirements. The following foods are suggested as suitable:—

Cocoa, Flour, Meat and Fish (in cans or in glass jars), Milk (canned or dried), Plain Biscuits (water, lunch, etc.), Suet or its equivalent, Sugar, Tea.

In storing foodstuffs selected from the above list, householders should see that:—

(1) Storage space is dry and cool.

(2) Any goods not purchased in cans, jars or airtight containers are placed in clean dry tins with tightly fitting lids.

(3) Biscuits are fresh and dry when placed in store.

(4) Articles are labelled with the date of purchase so that the stock never contains anything more than three months old : flour and suet should be used and replaced freq

These foodstuffs will not keep indefinitely. It is best to replace the stock regularly and to replace what has been withdraw earliest purchases can be withdrawn for use.

COUNTY BOROUGH OF SOUTHAMPTON. • **GOVERNMENT EVACUATION SCHEME**

EVACUATION
WILL TAKE PLACE ON FRIDAY & SATURDAY,
SEPTEMBER 1st and 2nd

THE SCHEME COVERS ONLY—

Schoolchildren (private, elementary and secondary).

Teachers and registered helpers.

Children under 5 if they are accompanied by the mother, or some other adult in place of the mother.

Expectant mothers.

Blind persons and cripples (not chair cases).

All those who are in these classes and wish to be evacuated, whether they have given their names in or not, MUST report at one of the assembly points given below, at the time and on the day stated.

Note: 1.—In the case of a family which has schoolchildren the assembly point should, if possible, be one of the schools at which the children attend, otherwise it should be the nearest school.

2.—A schoolchild who comes to school on the day of evacuation for that school will be evacuated. If you do not want the child to go, keep him or her away from school.

3.—Be in time.

4.—Bring gas-mask, food for the journey and a change of clothes. One bag only for clothes.

1st day. Friday, Sept. 1st, 1939		2nd day. Saturday, Sept. 2nd, 1939	
Bitterne Park Boys	Not Later Than 6.0 a.m.	Highfield C.E. / Swaythling Senior Girls	Not Later Than 6.0 a.m.
Bitterne Park Infants / Freemantle Boys, Girls and Infants / Ludlow Road Boys, Girls and Infants / Mount Pleasant Girls and Infants / Northam Infants / St. John's / St. Anne's Secondary School	Not Later Than 6.30 a.m.	Bassett Green Infants / Bassett Green Junior Boys / Foundry Lane Girls and Infants / Springhill R.C. Boys, Girls and Inf. / Swaythling Infants / Western District Boys and Girls / Atherley School for Girls / Grammar School for Girls / King Edward VI School / Taunton's School	Not Later Than 6.30 a.m.
Ascupart Girls and Infants / Bevois Town Boys, Girls and Infants / Bitterne Park Girls / Bitterne C.E. Infants / Bitterne Manor / Deanery Boys and Girls / Eastern District Boys and Infants / Merry Oak / Pear Tree Green / Sholing Girls / Woolston Boys, Girls and Infants / Woolston R.C.	Not Later Than 9.0 a.m.	Aldermoor Junior Mixed / Bassett Green Junior Girls / Central District Boys / Chestnut Road Boys / Coxford Girls / Foundry Lane Boys / Laundry Road Infants / Portswood Girls and Infants / Regent's Park Boys and Infants / St. Denys Boys, Girls and Infants / St. Jude's C.E. / St. Mark's C.E.	Not Later Than 9.0 a.m.
Bitterne C.E. Boys and Girls / Mount Pleasant Boys / Northam Boys and Girls / St. Joseph's R.C. / St. Mary's C.E. / Sholing Boys and Infants / Station Road	Not Later Than 12 noon	Aldermoor Infants / Central District Girls and Infants / Portswood Boys / Regent's Park Girls / Shirley Infants, Junior Boys and Girls / Shirley Warren Senior Boys and Girls / Western District Infants	Not Later Than 12 noon

IF YOU ARE NOT BEING EVACUATED, WILL YOU PLEASE KEEP WELL OUT OF THE WAY AT THE ASSEMBLY POINTS AND THE RAILWAY STATIONS.

ASSEMBLY POINT FOR BLIND PERSONS AND GUIDES — 43, THE AVENUE
On FRIDAY, SEPTEMBER 1st, at 9 a.m., Ready for Immediate Evacuation.

Evacuation time-table issued by the Authorities - Southampton during the week beginning 28th August 1939

'We were told what to pack in one small case: a change of underwear and socks, blouse etc., not too much to carry as in a shoulder bag we had our lunch and on the other shoulder our gas-mask. We walked six abreast up Campbell Road, Bow, to the Underground Station. My Dad was a Funeral Director and waved to me from the shop window. To me it was a great adventure.

Our teachers kept an eye on us all as some were prone to sickness, having started on their lunch too soon!

We changed trains, main line, and watched all the stations wondering when we were going to be told we had arrived. Our destination was to be Oxford. On arriving at the station we all went on buses to Summertown. We sat on a large green on Cutteslowe Estate and were given biscuits, corn beef, a tin of milk and a bar of chocolate....'

A.G. Leominster

'We formed up outside the school (St.Ethelburgers R.C.) with our gas masks, cases or carrier bags, a label tied on our jacket saying who we were. It was chaos, the noise, children shouting, mums crying and scolding their children at the same time to stay still and keep quiet. Other ladies trying to get us into groups to get us onto the coaches or, as we called them, charabancs. Once on, heads went out of the windows calling to Mums and others with arms waving. So, shouting our heads off we left Barking on a journey that was for most of us to change our lives forever'.

B.B. Romford

'Yes, this was the off. We smaller boys were at the head of the column. On our jacket lapel was tied a luggage label, the sight of such a label always stirs up so many memories, it has become the evacuees emblem. We were labelled parcels of the impending war, the distribution and destination of a Pied Piper exodus of epic proportions. Two girls held the poles of a small banner with the name of the school and evacuation party number printed on it.

My eight year old brother's case was carried by the head mistress, Miss Ambler. Passing through the large gates we spotted our mother on the far side of the road. Word had gone around on the grapevine.

A large policeman walked in front of us, we felt so important when he held up the traffic for us to pass. Some thirty minutes later we climbed the steep steps of Queens Road Southern Railway Station, some people tripped on the stairs.

My memories of the train journey are of being tightly packed on bench type seats. No corridor, so no toilet, the carriage compartments were open above the seat backs and we could hear the other children and teachers voices, singing was encouraged.....We ate our sandwiches, someone was travel sick, and I fell asleep with my head on a girls lap'.

J.R. Dartford

'Sitting on the 'charabang' (sic) outside St. Werburgh's Church, Birkenhead as a 6 year old was both traumatic and exciting. The day had come! or weeks we had been taking the clothes to school that had been listed as being 'essentials', 3 pairs of knickers, 3 vests, 2 petticoats, 2 night dresses (made from flour sacks), 2 jerseys, 2 skirts, 1 frock, strong shoes and 3 pairs of socks. Dad made our haversacks from pillowcases. We were also required to take gas mask and identity card. We were all tearful. My Dad had started us singing 'It's a long way to Tipperary' and by the time we had finished the song we were well on our way. I don't remember much about chattering, in fact we were very quiet. We arrived at the village hall in St. Martin's, Shropshire. We were no longer individuals, we were names read off luggage labels on our coats'.

R.C. Birkenhead

'I was nine years old when I was evacuated as a pupil of Mersey Park School. Birkenhead to Machynlleth, (now Powys).

I remember the teachers coming around the train encouraging us to sing-a-long, 'Daisybelle', 'Knees Up Mother Brown' and Gracie Fields 'Wish me Luck as you wave me goodbye'. I was amazed to find that the teachers behaved like ordinary human beings, talking to each other, calling each other by their Christian names, instead of Mr or Miss, and actually smoking!'

E.W. Birkenhead

'My earliest memories of evacuation are going to Dagenham Dock and getting on a boat which took us to Yarmouth. We were given straw sacks to sleep on in a large hall. On the Sunday morning my sisters and I, along with

23

my Mother, were sitting on Yarmouth beach. When war was declared my mother started to cry. Shopkeepers threw buckets and spades onto the beach for us'.

D.L. Romford

'The train journey was very long. This would have been around June 1940 and there were lots of troop movements. Us shunted into sidings at various parts of the journey and troop trains going by, one after another, they all waved to us...We got to Halsworthy in Devon and we were taken out. We were put in cattle pens originally, but I don't see why people are so upset about that. I can't think of a better way of containing children myself. I mean it was a lot of children to cope with and people totally inexperienced.

I got stung by a stinging nettle. I hadn't ever come across anything like that, it really hurt, I actually thought a snake had bitten me. This lady chucked down these huge green leaves and said 'rub it with that, cheal!'.

I.C. London

'I remember the excitement and fear about war. We heard so many terrible things about being evacuated. We had medicals and our heads looked at. One friend said she was going to Canada. I was jealous because I couldn't go. I never saw or heard of her again.

We were sent to North Wales by train. A label on our coat, gas mask and clothes in a pillow-slip. I was the eldest. We went to Abergele. Susie and John went to St. Aspaslt. They were very happy there. I stayed in Abergele with another girl Mary McMahon. We lived in a beautiful big house with a lady called Miss Mason. She was good to us...good food. It was the first time I had tasted Cornflakes. She had a maid called Linda. Linda carried all our food on trays covered by a silver cover. There was a lovely garden and fruit trees. Mary went home and I became homesick.

My mother was in Prestatyn. She had my little brother George with her and she was billeted at the Golf Club as she was having a baby'.

M.A.W. Liverpool

'1st September 1939.

After a late morning School-dinner, we were off. First a walk from Devonshire Drive, Greenwich to Lewisham Station. We were each issued with a carrier bag, with string handles which cut into the fingers and which contained our emergency rations. We peered in with much interest...one tin of corned beef, one tin of condensed milk, no tin opener, 2 packets of Ships biscuits which were discarded after their hardness had broken one tooth and pulled out a couple of fillings and, joy of joys, a half-a-pound slab of Cadbury Dairy Milk chocolate. Once we got to the station the chocolate was collected by the teachers for 'emergency use'. We didn't see it again.

I had imagined that the mind would be occupied by patriotic thoughts during the walk. Mine was only aware of the badly repacked rucksack with the heel of my first pair of high heeled shoes (at least 1½ inches) digging into my back. Getting away from the station fairly quickly the train meandered through the south-east countryside and eventually arrived at Battle Station.

Here we were ushered into a very large bus garage, somewhat smelly and with the floor covered in oil and grease, so there was no chance to rest the rucksacks or to squat down. It was a vast garage with only one door open so it was last in first out. We were the first in. Someone had a watch and when we finally got out we found that we had been there for 3½ hours. Food and drink was not available. When we were finally hustled onto buses we were past caring.

.......I was one of 12, from the same class taken to Sedlescombe with 2 members of staff.....We were to go to 'The Barn' but this was no ordinary barn but an attractive rustic building where the lady of the manor held her receptions. A large hall with beds at one end, a stage where the teachers sheltered behind heavy curtains, lavatories, wash basins and a kitchen behind the stage and outside its own charming garden.

The meal quickly appeared. It was now 9 pm. We had had nothing to eat or drink since late morning so anything would have tasted good as did the mince and bananas provided. Beds were quickly sought and within minutes all was quiet. Then ping, ping ping wallop. The beds, rough wooden frames with chicken wire tacked over them, were gradually collapsing. We all spent the night sleeping the sleep of the dead completely unaware that we were on the floor!'

D.T. Reading

'I was evacuated on September 1st 1939 with other children from London. My own particular school was Ecclesbourne Road Senior Boys School in Islington, quite near the Angel Islington. We were two schools in one building, the Ecclesbourne Senior Boys and the Ecclesbourne Senior Girls, although both within the same building, quite separate under a Headmaster for the boys and a Headmistress for the girls.

We assembled in the school playground at about 9 o'clock in the morning.....my memory tells me that there were about 200, maybe 250 children with our labels of course, our gas masks and some carrier bags and some with small suitcases. There was no trauma, we were generally a cheerful happy crowd and to many of us it was something of an adventure.

...We were marched in crocodile fashion accompanied by our teachers to Cannonbury Station where we very cheerfully boarded a steam train. The train proceeded from Cannonbury which is on the old North London railway, into Broad Street...I think we picked up the main LMS line to Bletchley and alighted at Bletchley about mid-morning and we again walked in crocodile fashion to the Cattle Market, quite close to the station. We were then organised and proceeded through some of the old

cattle pens and were issued with a carrier bag which among other things contained a tin of Carnation milk, a tin of corned beef, a packet of garibaldi biscuits and a post card.....We were then organised into large groups, possibly 2-3 dozen and taken by a couple of helpers and hawked around the streets. That was when it became a little trying because in effect there had been no advanced publicity that we were arriving....there was a tremendously mixed reaction'.

D.P. London

'.....My parents agreed to Evacuate us again if the LEA promised that we would be well looked after. When September 3 came Dad had bought three rucksacks. They were packed with our clothing as per instruction sheet, luggage labels were attached to us and our luggage. Our name and address, school and our destination written on them. We waited, complete with gas masks, outside Kings Park School for transport.

That day London Transport more or less came to a halt, buses, coaches and trains had been commandeered for the evacuation of school children to all parts of the country. Trams were still running, carrying passengers to their places of employment. Along came a convoy of London Transport double-decker buses, we said our last goodbyes to our mother. Dad had gone to work, I don't think he could take it.

I felt bewildered, didn't quite know what was happening.....I was crying and holding John's hand, he wasn't crying, he just had a puzzled look on his face. Bob held his other hand. We clambered onto the bus. I remember I couldn't see Mum. She had got lost in the sea of mums trying to get a last glimpse. We were off. We arrived at Well Hall Station. We had passed lots of waving people on the way.

We were bundled on to a train and told to keep our luggage on our laps, also told not to eat any of the sandwiches or sweets that we had with us. Mum had packed an apple and wine gums because we were not allowed to have anything to drink. There were no corridors or toilets on these

LONDON'S EVACUATION COMPLETE

AND NOT A SINGLE CASUALTY

London's evacuation is being completed tonight, Mr. Herbert Morrison, M.P., chairman of the London County Council Emergency Committee, said to a reporter today that the last of the parties would be clear away tonight. They expected that the number to be evacuated today would be about 50,000.

"Between 5.30 on Friday morning and midnight Sunday nearly 600,000 people and children were moved out of London" said Mr. Morrison. This vast population has been transported to the sea without a hitch. It is remarkable that there was not a single casualty," he added.

Dorset Daily Echo
4th September 1939

trains. The train arrived in Paddington Station where we were transferred to another train bound for the West Country. It seemed as though all the journey had been worked out so that there would be as little changing as possible. The journey was very slow. I remember the train being shunted into sidings, then going into reverse to get us on to the correct line.

We arrived at Staverton Station just outside Totnes, South Devon and were ushered into a long narrow hall which, I was afterwards to discover, was the school hall partitioned off during the day into classrooms. It was very dark but quite warm. We were all very hungry, very tired and very lost. There were chairs and benches in the hall but not enough for all of us, those who couldn't find a seat sat in rows on the floor.

People began to come in to choose which children they would have. Obviously the farmers were looking for bigger and stronger looking boys. I did not have to wait long before my name was called, along with another boy two years older than me. He was called Kenny Brimmer. This was unusual as everyone else was being sorted like cattle. I can only assume that because of the promise made to my parents we had been sorted beforehand. A man appeared, took our luggage and in a very kind voice said 'Follow me, me old 'andsome'. That was the last time I was to see my brothers for 15 months. We didn't even have enough time to say goodbye.'

G.B. Kent

Some evacuees were relocated for various reasons and therefore had to make additional journeys during the war. The following extract is the account of one such evacuee who, having suffered from an asthma attack, was transferred from his billet in a small village called Cleobury Mortimer in Shropshire to a convalescent home in south Devon. In 1941, aged 13, he made much of the journey entirely on his own, handed on from helper to helper until he reached his destination.

'Due to my having an asthma attack and my teacher becoming concerned about my absence from school, he informed the lady of the local manor.....

Miss Tomkinson, the lady of the manor, recommended I should be sent to a convalescent home in south Devon for treatment, she being on the committee of the I.C.A.A., a children's aid association.

I was taken to Chilton, the manor house, by my teacher....I entered the house through the stable -yard door which opened into the kitchen where Ruth, the cook, took me to see 'Miss Dora' who was unwell and confined to bed. She was sitting up in bed and asked me to be seated. Peering over the top of her spectacles she told me how I would leave for south Devon the next morning and gave me instructions on how I was to travel. That night I slept in the bath of the upper bathroom and later I was to learn that the house had nine bedrooms; perhaps they thought I should be quarantined. Being asthmatic and from Liverpool did not afford me a clean bill of health.

The next morning I left Chilton with a lady friend of Miss Dora's who was returning home to Bude in a hired car with a driver. As the car sped on through frost covered country side the lady pointed out the Cotswold Hills.

I was taken as far as Temple Meads station, Bristol where I waited with my pillow case of belongings and a label pinned to my coat. I was soon spotted by a WVS worker who took me into the station which had suffered damage from an air-raid. Where once was a roof only the skeletal remains of the frame could be seen with heaps of debris piled on each side of the platform. However, the rails were still intact and soon a train squealed to a halt and I was told to board and continue my journey to Exeter where I was to wait on the platform for further assistance. Another WVS worker approached me at Exeter and put me on the train to Sidmouth Junction where I was to leave the train and wait on the platform. By now it was dark and an overwhelming feeling of homesickness enveloped me. A man appeared who was to drive me to the convalescent home of 'Knowle' near Sidmouth. The driver carefully picked his way along narrow roads and blacked out villages by the dim light of the masked headlights. Just before we reached our destination I was startled by a sudden loud rattle from beneath the car, which the driver explained was a cattle grid. I had never before heard of such things'.

D.B. Liverpool

'At the outbreak of war, in 1939, I was aged eleven and a pupil at Troy Town Elementary school in Rochester, Kent. My parents had decided that I should be evacuated and on the morning of September 1st, together with hundreds of my friends and fellow pupils, I walked the half a mile or so from the school to Rochester railway station.

We passed through streets lined with crowds of emotional mothers and relatives, seeing their children off to unknown destinations and hopefully, safety. At Canterbury we detrained and paraded round the station square to be issued with carrier bags of food, accompanied by strict instructions to hand the bags to our hosts on arrival as they would not have food for us at that time.

We then boarded coaches to take us to various destinations, still unknown. On examining the carrier bag we discovered that the contents included 2lbs of Huntley and Palmers custard cream biscuits, a tin of Carnation milk, butter, tea and a 1lb slab of Cadbury's milk chocolate. Needless to say the latter disappeared before we arrived at our new homes'.

J.H. Reading

This particular school made an impressive entry into the reception area!....

'Our school was 'The Alexandra Orphanage', Maitland Park. London NW3.

Discipline was strict, we were allowed out only on Sundays for 90 minutes, with an inspection before we left and again when we returned. That gave us just enough time to walk to Hampstead Heath or Regents Park and back. Our P.T. teacher was an ex-PTI in a cavalry regiment during the first world war, and he joined the school straight from the army. We were taught to march and counter march and every year at Fete Day performed a march past very similar to that seen on Horse Guards Parade for the trooping of the colours.

Then came the war. On Friday, 1st September, 1939 we were shown how our gas masks were to be slung correctly from the left shoulder. Then it was on to buses to Mill Hill Station, on to a train, not knowing to where, and finishing up at Bedford Midland Station. I suspect the local Bedfordians wondered what was happening. Most of the evacuees looked frightened and unhappy to have left home. Their bags and cardboard boxes containing their gas masks hanging limp on hunched shoulders looking completely lost. Not us! We formed into a column of threes, boys at the front, girls following, all marching in step; left right, left right, with hobnailed boots clattering along the main road, just as if an infantry battalion had arrived.

Bedford was paradise to us. We were billeted out in to the homes of local people. One or two to a household. We had never known such freedom. To be able to leave home for school in the morning, back home for dinner, back to school in the afternoon, finish school and then free until next morning. Marvellous. No wonder we thought the war was not such a bad idea!'

D.D. Dagenham

This correspondent was evacuated in July 1944 after the V1 attacks on South London.

'I remember it was a dull July morning. Hundreds of evacuee kids congregated out in the open and the nearest shelters in the basement of the town hall 300 yards away, that's at Wimbledon and we were conscious of the threat of doodle bugs appearing. There was a row of London Transport ST double-deck buses with their destination numbers missing, standing in the main Wimbledon Station forecourt. There were also some more of them parked down Alexandra Road. This is where we eventually got on our bus after hanging around and being marshalled by officials. Some of the mums, including mine, came up to King's Cross with us. The bus journey was dreadful and we were all very subdued. When it came to hanging about at King's Cross waiting to go and then finally getting on the train, it was gut-wrenching. I don't think I cried but I felt as if my blood had been drained and I was feeling like a wrung out rag. The bottom had dropped out of my world after we had said our goodbyes.

On the train going up my brother really had no idea how to make things better for me. A few women who came just told us to 'cheer up, you are well out of it now!'

We did not know what was in store for us and we just had to get on with it the best we could. We ate our jam sandwiches quickly and derived what comfort we could by eating food made by mum's hand. When I see the contemporary footage of evacuees leaving on trains at railway stations, they do not seem to convey the utter misery of what I felt at the time, at that moment bleak, dazed, empty, extremely apprehensive and anonymous. I

When circumstances necessitate the use made of the empty trains may not be strictly in accordance with the following programme. Locomotive Department to be prepared to adjust working of Engines accordingly.

FIRST DAY.

Train Number.		Empty Stock.		Loaded Train.		Destination.		Empty Stock returned for next day's working.	
		Acton Yard.	Old Oak Common.	Acton.	Ealing Broadway.				Acton Yard.
		dep. a.m.	dep. a.m.	dep. a.m.	dep. a.m.			dep. a.m.	arr. a.m.
101	L	7†15	—	—	8 30	Maidenhead	.. ..	9†30	10†35
102	L	7†30	—	—	8 39	Oxford	. ..	10†50	p.m. 12†30
103		—	7†30	From Paddington		St. Austell	.. ..		
104		8† 0	—	—	8 48	Chippenham	.. ..	p.m. 12† 5	2†30
105	L	8†10	—	—	8 57	Henley-on-Thames	..	a.m. 10† 5	a.m. 11†10
106		8†20	—	—	9 7	Frome	.. ..	p.m. 12†40	p.m. 3†20
107		8†25	—	—	9 16	Highbridge	.. ..	—	—
108		8†45	—	—	9 25	Dorchester	.. ..	—	—
109		8†55	—	—	9 34	Bath	.. ..	12†40	3†55
110		9† 5	—	—	9 43	Devizes	.. ..	12†45	2†55
111		9†25	—	—	9 52	Weston-super-Mare	..	—	—
112	L	9†30	—	—	10 2	Oxford	.. ..	12† 5	1†45
113		9†40	—	—	10 11	Taunton	.. ..	—	—
114		—	9†35	—	10 20	Bridgwater	.. ..	—	—
115		9†45	—	—	10 29	Swindon	.. ..	1†25	3†30
116	West London	10† 0	10 30	—		{ Totnes	..	—	—
						{ Kingsbridge	..		
117	L	10† 0	—	—	10 38	Slough	.. ..	a.m. 11†35	12†10
118		10†20	—	—	10 47	Trowbridge	.. ..	p.m. 2† 0	4†25
119		10†30	—	—	10 56	Weston-super-Mare	..	—	—
120		10†40	—	—	11 6	{ Watchet	..	—	—
						{ Minehead	..		
121		10†45	—	—	11 15	Axbridge	.. ..	—	—
122	L	10†55	—	—	11 24	Maidenhead	.. ..	12†25	1† 5
123		11† 5	—	—	11 33	Bath	.. ..	—	—
124		—	11† 5	—	11 42	Malmesbury	.. ..	—	—
125	L	11†15	—	—	11 51	Oxford	.. ..	2† 0	3†40
126		11†25	—	—	p.m. 12 1	Swindon	.. ..	—	—
127		11†35	—	—	12 10	Wellington (Som.)	..	—	—
128	L	11†45	—	—	12 19	Wantage Road	..	2†30	4†10
129		p.m. 12† 5	—	—	12 28	Banbury	.. ..	—	—
130	West London	p.m. 12† 0	p.m. 12 30	—		{ Teignmouth	..	—	—
						{ Newton Abbot	..		
131		12†10	—	—	12 37	Weston-super-Mare	..	—	—
132		12†15	—	—	12 46	Taunton	.. ..	—	—
133		—	12†15	—	12 55	Chipping Norton	..	—	—
134		12†20	—	—	1 5	Langport East	..	—	—
135		12†30	—	—	1 14	Uffington	.. ..	—	—
136		12†40	—	—	1 23	Weymouth	.. ..	—	—
137		12†50	—	—	1 32	Oxford	.. ..	—	—
138	L	1† 0	—	—	1 41	Newbury Town	..	—	—
139	L	—	1† 0	—	1 50	Bath	.. ..	—	—
140	L	1† 5	—	—	1 59	Culham	.. ..	—	—
141		1†20	—	—	2 9	Warminster	.. ..	—	—
142		—	1†50	—	2 18	Weston-super-Mare	..	—	—
143	L	1†50	—	—	2 27	Witney	.. ..	—	—
144	West London	2† 0	2 30	—		Dorchester	.. ..	—	—

L—Non-corridor stock.

Extract from the emergency evacuation programme
organised for the early part of the second world war by the Great Western Railway

33

Working of Evacuation Trains from Acton and Ealing Broadway—continued.

First Day—continued.

Train Number.		Empty Train.		Loaded Train.		Destination.			Empty Stock returned for same Day's Working.	
		Acton Yard.	Old Oak Common.	Acton.	Ealing Broadway.				Acton Yard.	
		dep. p.m.	dep. p.m.	dep. p.m.	dep. p.m.				dep.	arr.
145		2† 0	—	—	2 36	Bicester ..	..	..	—	—
146		—	2†15	—	2 45	Cirencester	..	..	—	—
147		2†10	—	—	2 54	Bruton ..	..	..	—	—
148		—	2†25	—	3 4	Bath ..	..	..	—	—
149		2†30	—	—	3 13	Andoversford	..	..	—	—
150		—	2†45	—	3 22	Wells ..	..	..	—	—
151		3† 5	—	—	3 31	Swindon ..	..	..	—	—
152		—	3† 0	—	3 40	Savernake	..	..	—	—
153		3†25	—	—	3 49	Bridgwater	..	..	—	—
154	L	3†30	—	—	3 58	Oxford ..	..	..	—	—
155		3†35	—	—	4 8	Weston-super-Mare	..		—	—
156		3†50	—	—	4 17	Shepton Mallet	..		—	—
157		—	3†45	—	4 24	Bath ..	..	..	—	—
158	L	4† 5	—	—	4 33	Henley ..	..	..	—	—
159	West	London	4† 0	4 30	—	Weymouth	..	..	—	—
160		4†10	—	—	4 42	Swindon ..	..	..	—	—
161		—	4†10	—	4 51	Devizes ..	..	..	—	—
162	L	4†25	—	—	5 0	Maidenhead	..	..	—	—
163	L	4†30	—	—	5 9	Theale ..	..	..	—	—
164		4†50	—	—	5 18	Swindon ..	..	..	—	—

L—Non-corridor stock.

NON-CORRIDOR SETS—FIRST DAY.

No. 1.

6†55 a.m. Southall .. Acton 7†10 a.m.
8.30 a.m. Ealing .. Maidenhead 9.0 a.m.
9†30 a.m. Maidenhead Acton 10†35 a.m.
11.51 a.m. Ealing .. Oxford 1.30 p.m.
2† 0 p.m. Oxford .. Acton 3†40 p.m.
5. 0 p.m. Ealing .. Maidenhead 5.30 p.m.
6† 0 p.m. Maidenhead Southall 6†25 p.m.

No. 2.

7†0 a.m. Southall .. Acton 7†20 a.m.
8.39 a.m. Ealing .. Oxford 10.10 a.m.
10†50 a.m. Oxford .. Acton 12†30 p.m.
1.59 p.m. Ealing .. Culham 3.15 p.m.
3†50 p.m. Culham .. Southall 5† 5 p.m.

No. 3.

7†15 a.m. Slough .. Acton 7†45 a.m.
8.57 a.m. Ealing .. Henley 9.45 a.m.
10† 5 a.m. Henley .. Acton 11†10 a.m.
1.32 p.m. Ealing .. Oxford 3. 5 p.m.
3†35 p.m. Oxford .. Slough 4†45 p.m.

No. 4.

7†40 a.m. Slough .. Acton 8†05 a.m.
10. 2 a.m. Ealing .. Oxford 11.35 a.m.
12† 5 p.m. Oxford .. Acton 1†45 p.m.
4.33 p.m. Ealing .. Henley 5.30 p.m.
5†50 p.m. Henley .. Slough 6†30 p.m.

No. 5.

7. 0 a.m. Paddington Hayes 7.34 a.m.
8†20 a.m. Hayes .. Acton 8†50 a.m.
10.38 a.m. Ealing .. Slough 11. 5 a.m.
11†35 a.m. Slough .. Acton 12†10 p.m.
1.41 p.m. Ealing .. Newbury Town 3.0 p.m.
3†30 p.m. Newbury Town West London 5† 0 p.m.

No. 6.

9†25 a.m. Hayes .. Acton 9†50 a.m.
11.24 a.m. Ealing .. Maidenhead 11.55 a.m.
12†25 p.m. Maidenhead Acton 1† 5 p.m.
2.37 p.m. Ealing .. Witney 4.40 p.m.
5†10 p.m. Witney .. Hayes 7†40 p.m.

No. 7.

9†55 a.m. Slough .. Acton 10†50 a.m.
12.19 p.m. Ealing .. Wantage Road 1.45 p.m.
2†30 p.m. Wantage Rd. Acton 4†10 p.m.
5. 9 p.m. Ealing .. Theale 6.10 p.m.
6†40 p.m. Theale .. Slough 7†30 p.m.

No. 8.

2†45 p.m. Southall .. Acton 3† 0 p.m.
3.58 p.m. Ealing .. Oxford 5.35 p.m.
6†30 p.m. Oxford .. Southall 7†30 p.m.

Extract from the emergency evacuation programme
organised for the early part of the second world war by the Great Western Railway

THE
reception

It is obvious from this account that some hosts were just as nervous as the evacuees. Rumours of the possible poor state of health and hygiene of the expected evacuees could not have helped!

'Staff in school reported to the billeting officer to be allocated. Prospective hosts had been told to arrive at the school at a specific time. It was our job to check these people and their assessments and to help calm them down as some were extremely nervous at the prospect of meeting and then housing children from London. There were rumours that the evacuees were coming from the dock and 'slummy' areas of London and there were all sorts of stories circulating about poor personal hygiene, revolting eating habits, dreadful social habits and low morals. By the time the bus turned up with the children hours later, most people were a bit jumpy to say the least!'

M.C. Reading

'In the hall of the Leasingthorne Miners Lodge we were stood in line and wives were already there to take their pick of the children. Most of them wanted girls, and Sarah was taken by a woman who didn't want two children which made me very unhappy. I was blubbing my eyes out by this time and trying my best not to. Those of us who were left were then marched along the row of miner's cottages, knocking on doors, asking people if they would take a child. I'd never felt so lost and unwanted'.

J.H. West Sussex

'After three hours travelling we arrived at Blaenau Festiniog on a typical rainy day. The town was surrounded by slate quarries. We were led into a hall on to a stage, then the locals chose who they wanted. I had a pal, Jim Foster, who was like a brother to me, he was picked but he refused to go unless I went with him. So Mr and Mrs Robert Jones accepted us both. We arrived at the Jones home, at first it was frightening, Mr Jones, the local coalman had curls under his cap like a judges wig. Mrs Jones wore

powerful spectacles like the bottom of a whiskey glass. Outside you could see trees up in the air by themselves in the mist. Jim and I decided to escape....We got about two miles out of town up a steep hill, known as the Crimea Pass, when a policeman on a push-bike asked us where we were going, we told him we were going to Liverpool. Anyway we were turned around and led back to the Jones'. Next day the sun came out and everything looked very different'.

J.B. Warrington

'Before we could go into the main hall we had to undergo an examination and have our heads looked at. Then we were told to go into the big hall. We got a drink and a sandwich, then told to sit down and look pleasant and smile. I was the youngest of three that day from our family Doreen (10), Joseph (8) and myself (6). The nurse came out and told my sister to go back in.

'Is your brother a breeder?'

My sister replied, 'Yes, but we are not'.

My brother's hair was cut or shaved right down to the scalp, which marked him as a nit carrier'.

At the end of the day we were the last children in the hall because no one wanted 3 evacuees. In the end we were separated. A young girl of 16 chose me, I later learnt that her parents knew nothing about getting a 'house guest' for the duration, but they welcomed me with open arms and told me they were moving from the village to a farm they had rented. This for me was the start of 5 wonderful years with these people but my brother and sister were not so lucky'.

R.C. Birkenhead

'After Dunkirk, before or just after the Blitz started I think, train loads of children arrived at Exeter, and all the authorities could find us to do (as Scouts) was to 'escort' children on the Corporation buses as they were taken from the railway station to the housing estates (Whipton) where they were handed over to the people they were to live with. All that meant was that we stopped them from falling off....they were too tired and sad to argue or fight'.

I remember one bus driver calling out so that all could hear 'and this lot are all bedwetters'....What a start! What a welcome! You can imagine how keen the local people were to take those! What a daft thing to say!'

A.S.D. Reading

'Saturday Nov. 18. 1939.

Putrid day. Rain, rain, rain from a leaden sky. Had to receive an 'evacuee' at the station in the afternoon. Waited until four then they rolled up in a car. Took them to Edby and found kid's billet. Felt sorry for him. Bravely kept the tears back when he said goodbye to his father'.

From the Diary of E.A. High Peak

'Evacuees, or 'vaccies' as we were called, among other things, were looked down upon by many of the local children. To them we were noisy outsiders who had rudely disturbed their peaceful existence. Still, it had never been our wish, or even our decision, to invade their village. So the battle lines were often drawn as hostile encounters with village children pitted 'them' against 'us'.

M.K. Ontario

THE hosts

'I was delighted to hear that my new billet would be shared with an old school pal. I wasn't so pleased when I got there. It was miles out of town up a mountain road and next door to an abandoned burial ground. Here our hostess did her best but as she was very large and the live-in grandmother was the fattest woman I had ever seen, it wasn't easy. Going to bed was usually an ordeal. There was no black-out upstairs so that there was nothing to do but look out on the huge, white stone angel until grandmother began to snore, wheeze and whistle throughout most of the night. But by far the worst part was getting to and from school. Going down a rough stoney road did not make for speed and at the end of the day the road was too steep for anything other than bike-pushing. We were nearly always cold and frequently wet. To the billeting teacher, when asked for a move, we were just a couple of moaners unappreciative of the generosity of those who were keeping us from the bombs. On one of the rare fine days the same teacher trudged up the mountain to prove to us that the journey was perfectly reasonable. When she arrived the hostess and grandmother were sprawled on sofas idly watching the family dog playing on the carpet with a large lump of tripe. Apparently, offal was more offensive than getting wet every day and we were soon found new billets'.

D.T. Reading

'There was a lot of talk and consideration of sending children away to Canada or Australia etc. and my two cousins very nearly went. Instead they came and lived with us, that is, with my Parents, brother and sister, in Exeter. They lived in Southampton. Later, my grandparents, from Bristol, came as well which is why we didn't get 'proper evacuees' billeted on us. No room!'.

A.S.D. Reading

'At Locking Road School, we dispersed into several classrooms and were given bread and jam and tea. By then a number of children were rather fractious but.....I still seemed quite buoyant. There were no would-be foster parents there choosing their future guests, as I believe happened at some centres, but slowly the number of children seemed to dwindle as they were presumably carried off by car to their billets'.

A.K. Nottingham

'Soon we were being driven along a lane that took us right out of the village and then along a bumpy track. The driver didn't say very much except to tell us he was not the billeting officer. The car stopped near a cottage that looked like a picture on a chocolate box, except the garden was overgrown and weedy. When a woman (the housekeeper) opened the door our driver said, 'I've brought you two temporary foster children'.

To which she replied, 'Well, you can just take them away again. I never said I would have any evacuees'.

Undeterred, he pushed us into the house saying, 'According to our lists you have a spare room with a double bed. By law you cannot refuse to have them'.

With that he ran to his car and drove away quickly, leaving us standing there miserable.

The woman was very angry. 'They have no right to dump you on me. I have no food and the shops are miles away. What he will say when he finds out I don't know'.

J.R. Notts

ADVICE TO THOSE
TAKING EVACUEES

People who receive unaccompanied children will be expected to control and care for them as if they were their own. Should difficulty arise the billeting officer should be consulted.

Payment of 10/6 a week will be made for one child, or 8/6 for each child if more than one is taken. This covers full board, lodging, and all the care that would be given to a child in its own home.

*　　*　　*

For children under school age, accompanied by their mother or responsible adult, householders will be asked to provide lodging, access to water and sanitary arrangements, and it is hoped, cooking facilities. For this a weekly payment of 5/- for each adult and 3/- per child will be made.

Payment will be made weekly in advance at the local Post Office on a form supplied by the billeting officer.

*　　*　　*

Children and those accompanying them will receive Government emergency rations to cover the first 48 hours. Only minor purchases should be made at shops during that period.

Children will have hand luggage with a change of clothes. If clothes, boots or shoes need repairing the billeting officer should be notified.

*　　*　　*

In the event of the children becoming ill the local doctor or nurse should be sent for, but people with whom they are billeted will not be expected to pay.

*　　*　　*

The local education authority will be responsible for carrying on the education of evacuated children, and householders should see that they are sent to school at the arranged times.

In the case of unaccompanied children, the teachers will be near and able to assist in their control.

*　　*　　*

In order to occupy the children during their free time and so to help householders, local juvenile organisations will be arranging communal recreations. It is hoped that handicrafts and outdoor pursuits, such as gardening, may be encouraged.

So that a child may be kept healthy and happy the diet must be well balanced with plenty of variety. Baths should be given as often as possible, but at least once a week. Bedroom windows should be kept open at night.

*　　*　　*

As the children will be in strange surroundings and may be homesick, householders are asked to watch them carefully.

Householders are recommended to buy and store now an additional week's requirements of certain foods, and in doing so the number of children expected should be borne in mind.

Dorset County Chronicle, 31st August 1939

E R

I WISH TO MARK, BY THIS PERSONAL MESSAGE, my appreciation of the service you have rendered to your Country in 1939.

In the early days of the War you opened your door to strangers who were in need of shelter, & offered to share your home with them.

I know that to this unselfish task you have sacrificed much of your own comfort, & that it could not have been achieved without the loyal co-operation of all in your household.

By your sympathy you have earned the gratitude of those to whom you have shown hospitality, & by your readiness to serve you have helped the State in a work of great value.

Elizabeth R

Mrs. Hedges.

A copy of the printed personal message from H.M. Queen Elizabeth, was sent to all householders who took in refugees

billets

Dorset Daily Echo, 8th May 1940

Some evacuees were sent to very isolated billets as this account describes:

'There wasn't any shops in the village and Aunty went to the next village, Leigh upon Mendip, once a week to collect our rations. Twice a year she and Uncle went into the nearest Town, Shepton Mallet, to buy other essential items, mainly with the dividend she received from using the Co-op. Clothes had to be bought with clothing coupons and all the clothes were mended and passed down to each member of the family. Sometimes a man would come from Shepton Mallet with shoes and other clothes to sell from a suit case'.

N.C. Welling

(Evacuated to Leasingthorne)

'For an eight year old who had never been away from home, and then taken to live with strange people with their different way of living and a strange way of talking, was a great shock till I got used to it. They had outside lavatories called netties which were shovelled out once a week by a man with a horse and cart.

By the time we were billeted that night, it was dark and as I was desperate to go to the lav, they pointed me in the direction of the netty. It was pitch dark inside and felling around for the lav, all I could feel was a wooden bowl about 3ft wide with a flat wooden top. By that time I couldn't hold out much longer, I did my business on top of the box. It was found later what I had done, much to my shame. How was I to know you were supposed to lift the great heavy lid, where there was a second board with a round hole in it. I was told, the lid was there to keep the rats out, which didn't help my confidence one little bit!'

J.H. West Sussex

'....I received all the love and attention that Mammie and Jack could give me. It was a fantastic childhood, so carefree, with all the freedom that living in a very small village brings. Beulah had one sweet shop, a post office/village stores, a cattle feed merchant, petrol pumps, a chapel and of course the village school where we learnt to speak Welsh.

The house did not have electricity, gas or running water, we used candles and oil lamps and went to collect the water from the pump in the school playground. The cooking was done on an open fire, we had a range which had an oven beside the fire and I can well remember the lovely smell of freshly baked bread, tarts and Welsh cakes that Mammie made on baking day. She cooked the Cawl (*) in a very large black cooking pot with a handle across and this used to hang on a chain over the fire'.

J.H. Upminster

(*) Stew.

'We lived in a stone built cottage, 2 up - 2 down with a galvanised back house attached where all the washing and bathing was done. No electricity, only 1 oil lamp. No water indoors, only a cold water tap outside in the garden by the roadside. We used to clean our teeth outside under the tap using Gibbs Tooth Powder compacted in a little round tin. We bathed in a big tin bath with water heated in an old copper that you had to light a fire underneath. No cooker, only a fireplace with a little oven at the side which was blackleaded. Auntie cooked lovely meals on this fireplace. My favourite was Suet Pudding, any kind. Fruits and vegetables were all picked from the garden. Auntie must have worked real hard digging and planting in the garden to feed all of us all the year round. I can see her now digging in the garden when we arrived home from school. We had bantams in a pen up the paddock to give us fresh eggs, the large ones we got from over the farm, with milk in a jug straight from the cow, sometimes still warm. We often watched the cows being milked.

No indoor toilets, there was a bucket with a wooden seat across in a little wooden shed halfway up the garden, so pots under the bed at night and a hole in the garden dug to empty the bucket when it was full up. No toilet paper to be had, just squares of newspaper.

We had a walk-in stone larder which kept our food nice and cold and in which we had lots of fun catching mice with stale cheese loaded onto mouse traps.

We had no radio or music, but never missed it...Once a month a little van from Shaftesbury came down to us and we were able to chose our sweets with the coupons from our ration books'.

J.C. Chichester

'I was evacuated to a lovely village called Bontnewydd, near Caernarvon. It was a picture postcard village, containing a Post Office, small grocery store, dressmaker, Welsh Chapel, Welsh School and a Water Mill.

Although my placement was with a strict and childless couple, they were extremely kind to both myself and my family. After the war, and for the whole of their lifetime, they were like a second set of parents to me. Throughout the years I spent many long holidays with them. It altered my life considerably. Their standard of living was far higher than my parents could afford. They wanted to adopt me, but my parents naturally refused'.

D.K. Winsford

'I recall a great many tears being shed when our parents told us one Sunday morning that we were to go away to a place of safety, as it was too dangerous to stay in Dover, and our pleading not to be sent away were in vain. My next memory was of a very long train (from Dover), mostly in the dark and the blackout, until we arrived at a place called Ynysddu, near Blackwood in Monmouthshire, complete with gas masks and luggage identity labels. There, some of us disembarked but not my sister who went on to Blackwood. At the station an enormous policeman in Sergeant's uniform bore down on us and said 'I'll take him'. I wondered what I had done wrong, especially as I was taken to the police station, but I need not have worried as I was to become part of a larger family comprising two girls, one of my age, another older and a boy younger than I.

I spent three happy years with the Parry's, most of the time roaming the 'mountains' and playing in the coal-black river the Sirhowy. In bad weather we played darts in the police-station office or with the two or three revolvers (Webleys or Colts?) that were kept behind the desk. Occasionally a prisoner would be brought in and locked in a cell, an object of great curiosity for us all; some were described as 'deserters' and were eventually collected by more soldiers and taken away. We were not allowed to talk to the prisoners. At least once a year, having saved up the petrol that was rationed, we set off in a Standard car across the mountains towards Aberystwyth where Mrs Parry's parents kept a farm. Here the food was different, with home-cured ham, white butter churned on the farm by hand, clotted cream and dishes of broad-beans and blackcurrants. We were also allowed to ride the farm horses'.

M.E. (no address)

'...the lady at No.28 took me in. I think it was the idea of extra money coming in that prompted her as I was taken in under sufferance. My sister, in No. 32, was extremely happy while I was ignored most of the time, left out in all weathers, not allowed to play with my toys and when I was allowed to play it was in an outhouse which I can remember was very cold. Then I started wetting the bed and having nightmares. I must say that I cannot remember being smacked but that woman had a wicked tongue and told visitors that I was from Liverpool, I was not used to having baths and more or less said that I came from nothing. She could not have been further from the truth as I came from a lovely home albeit with a tin bath and a lavatory at the bottom of the yard.

After one year, this woman decided to take me home. I remember it was on a Monday morning....We caught the train to Liverpool, arrived at my home. My mother was doing the weekly wash in the shed where she kept the Dolly Tub and Boiler. I know a row ensued as the woman was asking for her train fare and my Mother was saying that she had been paid for my keep for that week. I think that day must have been one of the happiest days of my young life. My Mother sent for my sister soon after, even though she was happy to stay, but Mum said that we should be together. All of this happening during 1940, well before the terrible raids which came later'.

M.F. Bootle

'I was billeted with a family named Mayers....in a tied cottage belonging to a Farmer Bates for whom Mr Mayers worked as a farm-hand. It was to that farm that I was drawn, like a magnet, at almost every waking moment outside of school hours, where I spent the most exciting time of my life doing things that town boys dream of, driving horses and carts, haymaking, cutting kale and all the interesting things that happened on farms in those days...'

R.M. Merseyside

'The third move was a very unhappy one. I shared a room with another girl, but the lady of the house was very unkind, even cruel, and we were hungry. We had to sit at a table with a piece of bread and 'scrape' on our plates while the family ate a good cooked meal. The four year old once asked...

'Mummy, why don't you give the girls a lovely breakfast like mine?'

The answer was...

'Your Daddy gives me more to keep you than the billeting officer gives me to feed them'.

But, like most children at that time we told no-one. It was not until we went home for our holiday that our parents noticed how thin we were.'

K.G. London

'Feb. 20. 1940.

Mom (sic) saw me off at the station. ....Trains late, so we missed the connection at Gloucester. Had to run a special train. Dinner ready when I got in. Beautiful dining room. Lace mats, serviettes. Silver plate everywhere. Huge side-boards. Everything bright and lustrous. This is certainly a high-class billet and they certainly don't starve...Breakfast not until ten o'clock!'

E.A. High Peak

This account is unusual in that this person was evacuated early in 1939, before the war had started.......

'There was only one billet that would take the three of us, Mr and Mrs L. both nearly retired and their son in his forties living at home. It was a three bedroomed terraced house and my brothers and I slept in one bed, head to toe.

Mrs L. had all the dealings with us. She gave us our food, our orders and our punishments. I don't remember Mr L. or his son ever speaking to us. Whatever Mrs L. said or did was law and everybody obeyed her including her husband and son.

Every day we had porridge for breakfast, tea to drink. Our packed lunch for school was sandwiches, either jam, paste or marmite. We were not allowed to wear our shoes until Sundays because of the repairs. We had to wear Wellington boots outside at all times. These caused sores on the backs of our legs, especially Johns. For tea after school we had sandwiches again, either jam, paste or marmite, the only cooked meal was on Sunday.

School was a marquee on the local cricket field where we sat in rows, cross-legged on matting. We left school at three o'clock each day arriving 'home' to find that the house was locked. Everyone was out until 4.30. If it rained it was 'too bad' so we decided to go round to the back entrance. I climbed the fence to let my two younger brothers in and we sat in the greenhouse until one of them came home, usually Mrs. L. She used the cane on all of us because I'd left the back gate open and because we were in the greenhouse where she had grapes growing. The next day a tent had been erected n the garden for us to go into with strict instructions to lock the back gate after us. Unfortunately the tent was not waterproof so we got soaked. There was an old table in the garden which we pushed inside the tent so we could sit underneath, it tore the tent so we got another caning. I wrote home every day telling them everything that had happened. We seemed to get caned every day for one thing or another, it didn't have to be very bad to get the cane, wasting food by leaving a sandwich was good enough.

John's legs had started to bleed with the canings. Mrs L. must have felt bad about it so she got her son to bathe and cream the wound. I started to play truant from school and got caned for that. I played truant again and again.

Standing in front of the toyshop in Ashford one day I felt a hand on my shoulder and a voice said 'What are you doing here?' I looked up and saw it was my mother. The Education Authority had been in touch and had sent for her. Before I could answer her she had pulled me into the sunlight and was looking at my hair...I was running alive with lice.

She took me to the billet. There was no-one there so we went to the school where she spoke to the Head. We picked up my two brothers, then went to the billeting office where she made a complaint, showed them our hair and our legs, left us with the education medical staff whilst she went to collect our belongings'.

'A great time'.

'We arrived at Coombe Farm, near Buckfastleigh, at about 9.30 that night. The farm nestled in a valley, the house was built completely of grey slate. Waiting for us were Mr and Mrs Webber, her father and mother Mr and Mrs Bonathon, whom we were told to call 'Granmere' and 'Granfer'. Granfer was totally blind, a really wonderful man, in fact the whole family were 'out of this world'.

That night was my first introduction to home-made turnip soup, it is still my favourite, which was to become a regular meal every Saturday lunchtime before we went to the 'pictures'. After feasting and bathing for the very first time in a tin bath in front of a roaring kitchen range, we were introduced to our bedroom, two very tired, very clean and very full boys.

Ken and I awoke to brilliant sunshine and the sound of machinery. Looking out of the window we saw a working water-wheel which pumped water to the reservoir on the hill, this serving the farms and surrounding cottages. After a real country breakfast and lots of questions from them, we went down into the farmyard to meet all the animals and collect the eggs from the chickens, turkeys and geese, a rare experience for a 'townie'. There were six piglets with their mother, three cows, two calves, one working horse, Masher, the biggest horse I've ever seen, two ponies, a small flock of sheep, A Welsh Collie called 'Fluff' and a herd of about twenty bullocks and heifers.

Me (G.B.), Mrs Webber, Mr Webber, Granmere and Kenny at Coombe Farm

Harry farmed about 60 acres. On his land was a slate heap about thirty feet high, a hundred yards of broken slate. About a mile away was a slate quarry and joining the two was a tunnel running through a hill with real railway lines. As a special treat Harry took us through the tunnel one night, each of us had a paraffin lantern. It was very exciting for a boy of eight. In the summer Mr. Webber used the tunnel for cooling butter and cream.

My stay at Coombe Farm was a boy's dream. Of course I missed my parents but on the farm there was always something to do, apple and cider picking, potato planting and picking, kale cutting, mangel-wurzel cutting, hay and corn harvesting. We would pick mushrooms off the ten-acre field for market, pick primroses and wild violets and making them into bunches, again for Totnes market as well as Newton Abbott and Ashburton.

Mum, Dad, Bob, John and Me (G.B.) at Coombe Farm

One of my jobs on the farm was to help Granfer cut the wood each day for the fire. He and I would walk down to the barn, he holding my arm, me leading the way. Inside the barn was a two-handed cross-cut saw and a wooden horse. We would put the logs on the horse, cut them into foot lengths measured by Granfer's hands. He would be on one side of the saw, me on the other, for that he would give me one shilling pocket money for the pictures on Saturday and sweets from the provisions van that came around twice a week.

G.B. Kent

'At the village of Saltwood, near Hythe on the Kent coast, our coachload of children alighted to be greeted by the Billeting Officers. We then set off in 'crocodile' formation on a long tour of the village, dropping off children at houses along the way. As dusk was falling the last four of us, including two of my close friends from home, trudged up a lonely lane and followed the Billeting Officer into the drive of a large, imposing Georgian house.

The front door was opened by a young housemaid named Daisy, in a brown uniform and white apron. She ushered us into the largest hall that we had ever seen where we were joined by Roberts the cook, a lovely slim elderly lady also dressed in brown uniform and apron. It appeared that the house was the home of the Rector of Saltwood Church and his wife.....

They all welcomed us with open arms. Madam had given up her studio on the top floor which was a very large room, the full width of the house, to serve as our bedroom. We had our own bathroom, adjacent to the bedroom which was sparsely but comfortably furnished. We handed over our bags of provisions repeating the instructions emphasised to us at Canterbury. Madam, Roberts and Daisy burst into giggles at our solemn words and sight of the contents of the bag.

I had fallen off my bicycle two days before I left home and gashed my elbow. My mother had dressed it and given me a note which I gave to Daisy which she showed to Madam. Immediately I was whisked away to her private bathroom where she bathed and dressed the wound again. It turned out that amongst her many activities she was Commandant of the British Red Cross in the area.

We spent several happy months with them during the 'Phoney' period of the war. Roberts and Daisy taught us to knit and embroider Christmas gifts for our mothers and the Rector was delighted to have four recruits for his depleted church choir. We also learned to pump the church organ and ring the bells on Sundays. The gardens and orchard of the house were a boy's delight to play in the Rector delighted in having us on hand to partner him on his putting green'.

J.H. Reading

'I was sent to stay with a Mr and Mrs Drew in a house called 'The Laurels' in Bodenham. Mr Drew worked as a bricklayer for the Longford estate and was an occasional lay preacher with the small non-conformist chapels which were a feature of rural areas in those days, and we went every Sunday to the Elim church in Salisbury, preferring the Shergolds bus to the Wilts and Dorset as they never left anyone behind no matter how full they were.

Hats were doffed whenever the lord of the manor, Lord Radnor, rode through the village.....The house at Bodenham had no gas, electricity nor mains sewage so lighting was by '100 candle power' oil lamps and many games of 'Happy Vaccies' with Mick Mudd, Mona Mudd and Rip Saw the carpenter, were played in the light of those lamps'.

A.B. Fowey

'On arrival at Pulborough, we got off the train. I was given a brown paper carrier bag containing emergency rations. Then it was into a large space with all sorts of metal railings, some canvas with buckets, lavatories for our use which were completely open.

None of us had had anything to drink since our breakfast, many hours before. Streetwise town children soon sussed out a water tap on a stand pipe, a great rush for a drink ensued. We later learnt that this was the cattle market and the tap was for a hose-pipe used to swill the muck away.

```
(Please return to Mr. M. T. Perks, Chief Billeting Officer,
preferably by your evacuee whose teacher will collect
these receipts.)
                         ─────

R E C E I V E D  from the Billeting Authority :-
New Form No.    ...E.68.7.34.3.......
Ratebook ref.   ......57./.2.146....
Name of evacuee  Albert, Kenneth, Edith  FISHLOCK
Amount payable  .25/.6........... Dated ...4/.1/.40.....
Notes,

     Newly evacuated fm London

        ( This may be a duplicate receipt)
     ═══════════════════════════════════

Signed  ........Mrs. FRICKER...........
Address  ...........6. Orchard Rd P'th,
```

Receipt of payment made for having evacuees*

* Notice in this area the teachers had the extra responsibility of collecting in the receipts from their pupils!! Just something else to do. See newspaper article on page 65.

By now we wanted to explore the place, but had to wait ages, so it seemed, while one single-decker bus running a shuttle service, slowly conveyed us to the village school. But the school lane was too narrow for the bus and we had to walk the last part of the way up a steep pathway called Monkey Hill. 'Nitty Nora', the village nurse, steel combs and a bowl of bright pink disinfectant, was our next ordeal.

So we sat, my sister, my brother and I squashed in a two-seater desk, by now tired, hungry and fearful. What was to happen to us? I can still hear the braying 'County' voice of the billeting officer as she barked out the surnames of the helpers. But who wanted to take three children? No-one it seemed. They called out 'Who wants to go on a farm?' Up shot my hand and, despite my sister's protest, and our mother's instruction that we were to remain together, I was taken away to a car'.

J.R. Dartford

Evacuee payment receipt

school

School Days at Stour Provost School, Dorset:-

'Some days we were lucky to get a ride of sorts into school by the milkman....He used to deliver milk in a big black open roofed car with big running boards each side with a trailer on the back to carry the milk. We used to help him by standing on these running boards and delivering the milk to the cottages along the way. There used to be about four of us who got a lift in this way.

....I started school in Miss Carter's class and I can remember her reading us stories of Brer Rabbit from strips of paper cut out of magazines.

We often had the 'Nit Nurse' come round to the school as we seemed to get a lot of livestock running around and we Londoners always got the blame. Auntie spent many an evening using a 'nit' comb and Dettol on our hair so it was painful for her'.

(The correspondent returned to London and when caught up in the 'Doodle-bug' raids returned to her billet.)

'...When I went back to school for the second time I was up in Miss Kenwood's class. I can clearly remember hating arithmetic, especially long division for which I was always made to sit there until I got it right, apart from that I loved everything else. We did country dancing to a gramophone that Miss Kenwood had to keep winding up with a handle by the side.

We went for long Nature Walks in the country lanes and Duncliff Wood, so I know most of the wild flowers by name and sight.

We used to put on gymnastic displays and, being in the senior class, I was also allowed to go to the cookery classes about once a fortnight, taken by coach to the big school in Shaftesbury. I can also remember at one time making a loaf of bread and seeing it rise to the top of the tin and that was before it was put in the oven. What we baked we could take home for Auntie and the girls to sample for our tea'.

J.C. Chichester

'As there were only a few evacuees in the area, everyone went to the Vestry to start with and eventually we went to the village school where we learnt to speak Welsh. I can remember taking my basin and wooden spoon to school in the winter months so that we could have Cawl, a lovely Welsh lamb stew'.

J.H. Upminster

'Our schooling was exactly the same as in London. We had to walk to different parts of the town for our lessons. We used to go to the Senior School for our cookery lessons where there was a domestic science room. Other lessons were in the school room of the Wesleyan Chapel in the town, some were at the Bridge Chapel room. We had our games lessons in the recreation ground, the British Legion Comrades Hut was also used for lessons and communal dinners.

After some negotiating the authorities managed to get us to have our schooling under one roof at the Tithe Barn, Hinton St. Mary. We were exceedingly lucky to have this accommodation. We had the playing field for our games and P.T. lessons and the pavilion was our Art Room. There was an upper and lower room where we had typing and Book-keeping lessons. The Tithe Barn itself had a stage which was ideal for our drama lesson and the barn was used for lessons as well'.

S.R. Gillingham, Dorset

'When we first arrived the locals wouldn't let us go to school with them, so we played on the beach in charge of a teacher for the first few weeks, that was great. We then used the Wesleyan Chapel Hall for lessons and later on us girls were put in charge of the Stennack School Cookery room. We older ones had to help teach the younger ones sometimes.

One day three of us ran away from school but we only got a couple of miles. This resulted in a long lecture, a loss of being prefect of the school and a letter to my parents. My parents brought their holiday forward and also gave me a lecture and explained about the bombing and how bad it was and to try to settle down and be good. She even suggested to Aunt Susan (host) that I helped around the house doing the dusting. I ended up doing most of the housework'.

G.F. London

Education could be problematic, especially for evacuated Jewish children.

'Aunty sent us to Sunday School in the morning and chapel in the evening. My mother did not object to this as she felt that everyone should learn something of other religions apart from their own. She also felt that there would be a lot less trouble in the world if everyone did this.

At school, it proved very difficult to learn anything as there were about 60 of us in one class as we were taught with the Cornish children. I remember we had a lot of singing lessons, mostly of very patriotic songs. We also had to do a lot of marching around the playground. The Cornish headmaster had been a Captain in the first world war. The London Headmaster was a Mr. Bristow and he had an assistant called Mrs. Phillips....

A Hebrew teacher came twice a week to teach the Jewish children. We were taken to a shed in the playground. I enjoyed learning Hebrew and received a prize for it. When it came to the Jewish festivals, particularly the High Holy days in September, we were taken to the Church of England in Sticker village where Jewish children from other schools were also taken and we celebrated the festivals there'.

S.B. Kent

'I believe there had been some assumption that I would go to the school for local residents but in fact I joined, or was directed to, the Rothschild Junior Boys' school evacuated from Acton, London. (The correspondent had been evacuated privately from Mitcham, Surrey). *The school met, initially, in the afternoons at the Colliton Street school. The local boys had it in the morning. Shortly afterwards the YMCA, then in Church Street, was added as a school venue and we alternated there, one week YMCA in the morning, Collington Street in the afternoon; next week the other way around, with the local boys. Yet we never mixed with the local boys. I don't think that had any significance than the fact that at that age one's friends tended to come from your particular school which in most cases was one's only social venue. I can recall no stigma, hostility or unfriendliness from anyone during my stay at Dorchester for being an evacuee. Collington Street of course offered a fairly formal school environment, typical of the times, but the YMCA was hardly ideal. I recall spending most of the time sitting on somewhat dated leatherette settees and armchairs, far too generous in size*

for nine year olds! Yet it was there that I first heard a school programme on the wireless, which seemed at that time to be an innovation without measure. (*) Despite all, I recall that the lessons were formal and positive and my report for Christmas '39 shows that we were tested in English, separately in reading, spelling, composition, language and writing, and in Arithmetic, mechanical, mental, and problems, besides Geography and History. The number in the class was 28.

A.K. Nottingham

* The BBC tried to keep schools broadcasting on the air. Although the printing of pamphlets which had accompanied pre-war programmes had to be stopped and some programmes such as Modern Languages had to be abandoned, by 1944 thirty-one weekly series, a daily news service and twice-weekly religious services were on offer. The number of schools making use of this service rose from 10,000 to 12,000. One head mistress wrote to the BBC stating that the broadcasts were 'like life-buoys in a queer, turbulent, scholastic sea'. (What did you do in the War Auntie? Tom Hickman. Pub. BBC 1995. p79)

'Starting school is a little bit of an exaggeration because school consisted of attending a multi-number main hall. The size of the hall can be judged from the fact that the alternative use for it was where they would hold plays for the school and this is when we were first introduced into some stage activity. Billy was given the part of Jiminy Cricket in the play Pinocchio. Another Liverpool boy, Harry McQuirk, was given the part of Pinocchio...'

V.M. Liverpool

THIS WEEK'S BROADCASTS TO SCHOOLS

The School broadcasts this week aim at providing bright and instructive fare for children between nine and 15 years, though even the juniors down to five are catered for in the 'Music and movement' series. In addition, the science and foreign affairs talks are intended for senior pupils.

A dramatised biography of Sir Walter Scott will be broadcast in the afternoon tomorrow, while the fourth of a series of biographical plays dealing with the life of Joseph will be heard on Wednesday afternoon.

Music lessons will cover a wide field. Christmas music will be the subject of John Horton's preparatory concert lesson tomorrow afternoon. Sir Walter Davies will give a fifteen minute lesson on music making on Wednesday afternoon and Ronald Biggs will deal with "Music for Every Day" on Thursday Morning.

Evacuated children should find special interest in the "Living in the Country" series. Tomorrow afternoon, Edith E. Macqueen will deal with the history of village inns and their strange names, John R. Alan will contribute to the series on Wednesday morning to talk about how farm animals are fed in Winter.

Other features of the school broadcasting week will include a lesson on autobiographies in the senior English series on Wednesday by S. P. B Mais: a talk on the "Geography of the War: Sea Borne Supplies," by A. G. Ogilvie on Thursday morning and a feature programme by Rhoda Power on the Spanish Armada on the same afternoon.

A boys life in Kenya will be dealt with in Mrs Elspeth Murray's travel talk on Friday afternoon and this will be followed by a topical feature programme entitled "Getting Your Fish in Wartime".

Sir Fredrick Whyte will complete the school week on Friday with a talk on foreign affairs for sixth forms.

Dorset Daily Echo, 4th December 1939

'I went to school in the village hall, but I never remember having any paper, pens or a blackboard and I don't remember learning anything'.

C. Liverpool

'....our classes had moved to the Church Hall. On a Friday afternoon we were able to just take games, or the teachers used to help us do various craft works, one of which was to knit balaclavas in Khaki wool, supposedly to send to the soldiers, but I suspect it was more of a ploy on the teacher's part to keep our fingers busy! On a Saturday we used to meet at the school and go rambling, and learning the names of the wildflowers and birds. Looking back those teachers must have dedicated a lot of time to our welfare'.

E.W. Birkenhead

'The village school had a range of ages in one class so we had a variety of lessons. Our needlework was 'make do and mend'. We also had garden plants to grow, radishes and sweet peas. I also did a cheese making course quite an experience for a London girl, but I enjoyed it all'.

A.G. Leominster

'The school I went to was at Alderbury and we walked the mile and a half along the main Salisbury to Southampton road to the turning off to the school called Silver Street. Some of our teachers came with us and I remember a Mr Short and Mr Lush. One of the local boys one day called him Mr. Slush and we watched in awe as a cane-wielding Mr Lush chased him around the classroom. We were tightly packed into that little school. I can remember chanting out the tables in those classrooms and was eternally grateful throughout my engineering career for being made to remember them. There were also sessions of mental arithmetic which those who could do it liked...

I have read later of the BBC putting on programmes to help the education of the evacuees, but we certainly had no access to a radio'.

A. B. Fowey

'.......it was deemed wise for us to be evacuated again. This time we went to a prep-school at Hartfield near Crowborough, Sussex. Wooden dormitories, classrooms and dining rooms had hastily been erected in the grounds and I spent several months in this quite delightful environment of Ashdown Forest.*

The tempo of our studies was interrupted from time to time by thousands of Australian and New Zealand troops who descended on the surrounding Forest for battle training. As a result we were provided with acres of slit trenches and dugouts in which to fight our own mock battles. Several boys were fortunate to acquire bush hats from friendly soldiers and they wore these proudly as they stormed the dugouts'.

J.H. Reading

'...For the first 5-6 weeks we shared the school with the local children. They attended in the morning and we attended in the afternoons, so we were getting half a day schooling. Subsequently we were virtually abandoned by both the Bucks C.C. and the L.C.C. ....we were banished. The girls to a Church Hall, probably 30-40 of them under one teacher and Head mistress, Miss Stern, and ourselves. Would you believe our school was in the cricket pavilion at Bletchley Park!......our schooling virtually consisted of reading, tending our little allotment in the 'Dig for Victory' campaign and cricket and football depending on the season, and a little bit of woodwork. My foster parents were so concerned about my education that they sent me to evening classes'.*

D.P. London

'School was five miles away from the farm at Landscove. The first day Dick Webber took us in his car, he used to collect the milk churns from the different farms taking them to the dairy. After that, we walked there and back. In the Winter in the dark, returning in the dark until we learned to ride, then we rode the ponies to school'.*

G.B. Kent

'In September 1943 I was moved to Ebbw Vale to join the Dover Grammar School which was billeted on Ebbw Vale County School and housed largely in a building known as the 'Tin Tabernacle'.*

M.E. Haverfordwest

'Our teachers had been evacuated with us so the local Catholic Church was used as a school. A partition was drawn across the altar and the benches were turned into desks. We went every day to school but as my younger brother and sister were only 5 it was decided that they would only go in the afternoons as this was a very long walk from the place we lived'.

M.H. Liverpool

'School work was ad hoc...no books and no equipment. The subject matter depended entirely on which specialist teacher could manage to get from one village to another. Geography and English specialists were nearby so we learned a lot about the Geography of the south-east of England. We also had reams of poetry quoted to us from memory. I can still recite the long poem..' From the troubles of the world I turn to ducks!'

D.T. Reading

'We didn't have far to walk to school, which was for infants and juniors and quite small. On window sills were glass jam jars with things growing in them. Blotting paper was circled around the inside and filled with sawdust. Peas and beans were put between the glass and paper and the sawdust was kept moist. You could watch as they grew, first the roots emerging and then the stalks and leaves. The school also had a small garden where we dug, raked, hoed and planted things in rows....A less than useful occupation was our efforts with raffia. We made tablemats, and long strips which were supposed to be belts and using bits of coloured darning wool and cardboard milk bottle tops, we made pompoms'.

J.H. West Sussex

'Autumn 1942-Summer 1944.

The main preoccupation for the next two years was schooling. I needed 4 separate Science 'A' levels and there was no single school to provide them. Chemistry was probably the most difficult. Taught individually, but with little practical work, it was interrupted by a 6 month illness of the teacher. Academic duties combined with billeting had taken its toll. Then it was at our Boy's School equivalent, where the teacher hadn't taught girls before and didn't like them. There, a very minor mishap in the Lab. gave him an excuse to get rid of me.

For Physics I went to the same school. The teacher, called out of a long retirement, had never taught girls in his life and was probably scared stiff of me. He solved his problem by completely ignoring me, refusing to see my flapping hand when I wanted to raise some point of clarification. After a year the boy's school went back to London and the second year was spent at a local Tech. working on a different syllabus and working on the same topics as had been studied in the previous year.

No nearby schools taught Botany and Zoology as separate subjects, so it was 4 miles up the valley to another evacuated school, working on a different syllabus and working on a combined course. After a year, this school also went back to London. Thus my second year of Botany and Zoology was spent at the local Grammar School with yet another syllabus and where most of the interesting topics were discussed in Welsh. I can only think that that years Examiners, knowing something of our problems were particularly lenient when marking evacuee's scripts'.

D.T. Reading

(Despite all her problems D. passed her exams and went on to the University of Reading.)

'We shared the village school. My sister was in a class with the local children. My age group from Coventry were taught in a separate building heated by a cast-iron stove, a common feature in schools then. No school dinners. Our packed lunch was slices of bread spread with home-made lard, and a bottle of milk mixed with cocoa powder which we were supposed to heat on the stove, but usually drank cold'.

D.R. Hemel Hempstead

'There were not any school dinners, we all had to take a packed lunch. At that time we used to have a drink of milk at morning break and in the winter this was put into a large saucepan to heat on the big black boiler that heated the classrooms. This boiler needed regular stoking and this was done by the teacher. After lunch we laid down for a rest'.

N.C. Welling

'One memory that remains is the way I learned the meaning of the word transplant. Whether it was a class nature exercise or part of the wartime 'Dig for Victory' campaign for home-grown vegetables, I have retained this blurred impression of myself kneeling on the ground at the side of the school putting some small seedling into the soil.

This seemed to be an encounter with nature and a vivid learning experience that completely fascinated my young mind at the time. I wonder if, subconsciously, I did see some similarity between that seedling and myself'.

M.K. Ontario

The following account is given in its entirety to show how complicated providing any semblance of a worthwhile education was!

'We returned to London at the end of the summer term in July 1940 and a few weeks later I started at the West Ham High School. I was somewhat overawed at the size and beauty of the building, it was so spacious and bright and polished. We had a school porter who wore a smart uniform and he and his wife ran a tuck shop at break times where we could buy biscuits or fruit or carrots!. It was a whole new world to me. There were new subjects to be learnt and new sports to be played...it was all very exciting.

Within a couple of weeks life changed completely for on September 7th 1940 the Blitz started on our part of London. That Saturday afternoon was horrific and when we emerged from our shelter we found our home badly damaged and we weren't allowed any where near it. The rest of the weekend was spent in and out of shelters or under the stairs in my aunt's house in Plaistow. On the Monday we left to seek refuge with my eldest brother-in-law in Wing, Bucks. We arrived on their doorstep unannounced and literally with only the clothes we stood up in.

After a few weeks, early in October, my father arranged for me to join a small group of West Ham High School girls who were in Faringdon, Berkshire. At last I began to have some schooling. We joined the classes with the Faringdon High, there were not enough of us to have separate classes. At this time there were still some girls in Stratford, some in Brentwood, where they shared the Ursuline Convent, and our group in

Faringdon. Sadly, our beautiful school was completely demolished on November 16th 1940 and this meant that the Stratford girls dispersed to other schools.

In the spring of 1941 we were told that all three groups would be moving to Truro in Cornwall, in the hope of keeping the school going. The girls from Brentwood moved on March 13th, Faringdon on May 3, and Stratford on May 6th.......

We were met by staff and billeting officers and were soon taken to our new homes. I know I felt tired and miserable. I was a shy child and it was an ordeal to have to meet new people and a new home, my fourth in 18 months. But, tired or not, school started the next day!

We shared the Truro County School for Girls. We had some classrooms but also used the corridors as classrooms. We had the use of the hall for assembly, music and gym. We did not mix with the County girls except when we played hockey, netball, rounders or tennis against them. I don't think I got to know a single Truro girl. Miss Carter, their Head., was very hospitable and did her best to co-operate so that the two schools could function smoothly. It must have been very inconvenient for them to have another 80 or more girls squeezed in to their school.

School went on as normal though we were often without teachers when they went to London to try to salvage things from the old school. We were pretty good and worked quietly on our own, but sometimes we got bored and fooled around. I had the job of time-keeper for our school. The County School used a bell to mark the end of lessons and we used a whistle. I had to keep an eye on the time, blow the whistle at one end of the building, then dash downstairs along the length of the building up more stairs and then try to find the breath to blow the whistle at the other end of the building. things were timed so that the two schools were never on the move at the same time. I realise now that this must have taken a great deal of co-operation from both schools, but at the time we just took it for granted.

It was a real joy to have playing fields attached to the school, the only thing we travelled for was swimming. Every Wednesday on the Summer term we would go from school down the hill to the station, take the train, change at Chacewater and on to Perranporth....and we grumbled! I'm sure most of the girls at the school would love the chance to go to such a beautiful place to swim every week. We had Sports Day at Perran and Newquay on their lovely firm sands. One memorable occasion was when we were about to have an egg and spoon race. We had no eggs so we used potatoes. These were put out in line while the girls were being lined up about 100 yards away. Just as the teacher was about to start the race a flock of seagulls swooped down on our potatoes....that was the end of that race!!!

I am amazed we did all the school things, plays, concerts, Red Cross classes, knitting for the Forces. We knitted up to 40.lbs of wool in our two year stay at Truro. We knitted pullovers, balaclavas, gloves, mittens, socks and sea-boot stockings. We were taught not to waste a minute, if we sat down, even to read, we had knitting in our hands. We also set up a National Savings Group and had fund raising events for Truro Warship Week, and the following year Wings for Victory Week.

A new activity for us was Arts and Crafts as opposed to drawing and painting, which I could never do. These classes were taken by Miss Asquith, a teacher employed by the LCC. The classes were held in rooms above a book shop in Boscawen Street. There we learnt to weave on small looms and large. I know I loved to work out the patterns for this. We made papier mache puppets and put on puppet shows for our school and visitors. Our out of school activities included a Red Cross group. We had talks and demonstrations and did practical work, eventually taking exams in which we all did well. I was very proud because I got a distinction. Once we reached the age of 14 we were allowed to go to Truro Infirmary on Sunday evenings when they were short staffed and we helped with the supper things, collecting the plates from the patients and doing the washing up.

We used to go home for some of the holidays and when the train approached Saltash Bridge we would gather round the window and raise a great cheer as we left Cornwall behind and on the return we did the reverse, we groaned as the train came off the bridge.

....With each holiday our numbers dwindled until July 1943 we were down to 65, below 60 and the school would not have been viable. We had a fierce loyalty to our school and were determined that a school which had been in existence for 176 years was not going to finish with us....In July we returned to London and were given some rooms in the Ursuline Convent in Upton Lane. Gradually girls returned and the school numbers

went up. It was good to renew old friendships and make new ones. When the flying bombs started we spent a lot of time in the shelters. We would leave the classroom, make our way to the shelter, take up our allotted places, open our books and continue as if nothing had happened. When the V2s started there was no warning. If there was a explosion which rattled, or even broke, the windows we had to ignore it and keep our heads in our books.

Looking back I appreciate the hard work, devotion and selflessness of our teachers. Our education continued, in spite of interruptions and difficulties. They were always concerned for our welfare and did their best to keep us happy'.

K.G. London

'The original Weston Boys' and Girls' County schools had near identical halves of a common, and by those days, very modern building. Any fraternisation between the schools was very heavily frowned upon. The dividing line was North-South. After the fire bomb raid when the girls half was destroyed, the evacuated schools went home and the local girls and boys had to share the same half, this rigidity was still maintained but this time on an East-West axis. However, this arrangement was much less watertight, being an enforced expediency. Crossing points had to be accepted and I am sure that if anyone could have foreseen the future, at least one such crossing would have merited the sobriquet 'Check-point Charlie'. To be held up there whilst the opposite sex were ushered past enlivened the day......

My wife's sister who was at the school before the air raid, remembers being admonished with other members of the class (Parents were asked to see the Head Mistress!) for leaving notes in the inkwells for the evacuated Barking Abbey Boys who occupied their classrooms in the afternoon'.

A.K. Nottingham

camps, hostels & residential schools

There were 32 Camp Schools around the country run by the National Camps Corporation under the aegis of the Ministry of Health. The following accounts describe life in three of them, and although they all had their individual characteristics there were similarities in the way in which they were organised. These accounts have been transcribed almost in full because they describe a part of the evacuation which few people know about other than those who were directly involved with the camp schools. The fourth description is of life in a residential school and again there are similarities between this institution and the camps.

BISHOPSWOOD FARM SCHOOL, SONNING COMMON

The first account is from an evacuee who went to a Camp School in South-Oxfordshire. He had originally been evacuated as a member of an orphanage to Bedford and remained there until February 1940.

'On February 26th 1940 the Senior Boys and Girls were moved from Bedford to Bishopswood Farm Camp, Peppard Common, near Sonning Common, Reading. Our camp was about 2 miles from another camp called Kennylands.....

Back in London boys and girls never mixed. We saw the girls in chapel every morning where they sat at the centre pews and we boys on either side and at the back. We also saw them at meal times where they were the strange creatures who sat on the other side of the central serving table.

At the camp things changed and we had mixed classes a thing unheard of before. We still sat separately 2 rows of 12 boys and 2 rows of girls. At last we began to realise the girls were as human as we were (if you could call us human). The fact that woods surrounded the camp also helped some of us to understand about girls! I can't ever remember speaking to one of them. There is not much doubt that I was a bit shy.

The Duchess of Kent (right) inspects residents of Bishopswood Farm School - May 1943
From left- School Matron, not known, James V. Rank (President/Chairman
of Board of Governors), Charles Fife (Head teacher),
Duchess of Kent (Vice-President of Board of Governors)

As one entered the camp by the main gate, on the left was the Headmaster's house and office and on the right a small infirmary run by the school matron. There were 3 boys dormitories, in each 40 boys sleeping on 2-tier beds. There was a master's room in each dormitory to keep control. On the far side of the camp there were also 3 huts, but only two of them were used as dormitories for about 60 girls. The third hut was used as a classroom for teaching such things as cookery and woodwork.

The main assembly hall, complete with stage, also doubled as a classroom for the older boys only. They had no teacher but sat and did revision of past work, liable to be asked for work to be shown at any time.

Another hut contained 4 classrooms, containing mixed classes. The only other building was the dining hall. On the end of this was the tuck shop. In the year I was there I can only remember it being open 3 times for about 2 hours.

Two of the masters and their wives and children lodged in Sonning Common, one of them stayed at the Post Office. Our PT teacher lodged at the local pub, which I believe was called the 'Woodman'. He was no fool!

We were allowed out for walks and on Peppard Common we met some local Boy Scouts. They introduced us to their scoutmaster. He visited the camp at our request and our own troop was formed. This was a great success with the girls forming a Guide Group.

Any children who passed the 11+ examination were bussed to Henley Grammar School each day.

I left school at Easter 1941 having spent 7.5 years at the orphanage and the school. Looking back I loved every minute of it. I think nobody could have had a happier time at school, in spite of the discipline, and I wouldn't have changed a second of it'.

D.D. Dagenham

(On 18 August 1996 D.D. returned to the school, along with 100 others, for a reunion of old scholars and the placing of a commemorative plaque. Only one of the original school buildings remained standing and this had been converted into a club room and bar. The rest of the area is now in use as football and cricket pitches.)

KENNYLANDS CAMP SCHOOL, SONNING COMMON

View of the entrance to Kennylands Camp

Kennylands Camp, was also in Sonning Common near Reading and just down the road from Bishopswood Camp. It was the first camp school and was built in 1940. This correspondent arrived there on 25 August 1942.

'My education seems to have ticked over without hiccups and I took the scholarship at 11, but although I did not pass, I was considered good enough for the Central School, Beal Modern, and then evacuated to Kennylands Camp. They went to Kennylands to be the first camp school in February 1940.

The camp consisted of a collection of wooden buildings on either side of a drive with dormitories on one side and administrative buildings on the other. On the left hand side of the drive the administrative buildings consisted of a dining hall and a kitchen, there was an assembly hall, a hospital, staff quarters, lavatory blocks, a camp manager's house, a boiler house and classrooms. On the right hand side it had 6 dormitories which were 3 one end and 3 the other end of a development with a splendid cricket ground dividing them. The layout was pleasing to the eye and the whole area was beautifully landscaped with the dormitories backing onto a huge playing field. My first day memories are of being shown our dormitory with its rows of bunk beds along each side and the whole housed about 36 boys. These were double bunks......

Life as a first former was not easy and we were subjected to any amount of bullying with bruises on arms and legs as par for the course. Our schooling however, seemed to have been very much on course and we hadn't suffered at all from the war. Our intake was divided into A and B classes with the A aiming ultimately for the Oxford School Certificate and the B for the RSA exam.

We lived a very enclosed existence and did not venture far from the camp, except on Saturdays when we were allowed to go to Reading. This meant seeing the Reading Football team or going to the cinema. There were only about 200 boys, 12 teachers and the headmaster, so one got to know everybody in varying degrees together with the camp staff.

......One of the penalties for wearing shoes in the dormitory, always definitely not allowed, would be a punching on the arm...the other way of dealing with you was to put you on fatigues and that meant cleaning the dormitory on Saturdays or you did the gardening, there was always a lot of gardening went on in those days.

One of the variations of bullying I can remember well was putting a boy in a laundry basket on the top bunk and pushing him down onto the floor so he went down with a thump. How anybody didn't get badly injured I'll never know. They were also quite fond of having people run the gauntlet and flicking them with wet towels which is quite a painful thing in the showers and not to be recommended. There were no bathing facilities, just showers and the ruling was you had to have one shower a week which was recorded in a 'shower book' kept by a Prefect. To get to the showers, or the toilets you had to go across the drive so in winter it wasn't much fun, and if you went in the middle of the night I don't quite know how you got on there...

The food was I think what everybody had in those days. It was things like sort of made up meals like 'Vienna Steak', Shepherds Pie was quite a popular one. Peanut butter for some reason was not rationed, that seemed to be quite popular and another thing was we used to make 'sauce sandwiches'. I remember having it just with sauce, HP sauce, but the meal above all other really sticks in my mind was the fish on Friday which was absolutely dreadful. It was some sort of steamed fish and we had 'pomme potatoes' which was a sort of powered potato and it finished up as a grey sludge. It was all covered in parsley sauce, it was absolutely revolting. (Legend had it that Lord HawHaw had mentioned this in one of his broadcasts and he said there was a school near Reading that was being fed on bad fish from America. I am not sure whether this is true or not but in fact I did speak to my old art master, now in his 90s, and he said it was true...so perhaps it was.)

The King and Queen visiting Kennylands Camp on the 30th September 1940

I remember Rissoles, that was another thing we used to have and they were very keen on giving you a balanced diet. I remember we had one lady teacher, Miss Cambridge, (we had to have lady teachers after a while because the men teachers were at war), and she used to be responsible for trying to keep the diet balanced and for some reason we could not get lettuces so we had cabbage instead, which wasn't a very good substitute....Actually having your meals was quite interesting because you used to have 6-8 boys on each table and one was in charge and all the others took it in turns to serve and there was in fact one famous occasion when the whole school went on strike and refused to go up and get their meals from the serving hatch because we had obviously for some reason had become dissatisfied with the food, but the whole thing collapsed when one boy broke the strike by going up for his food..so that was that!

There is no doubt that it was a wonderful place for sport... We had the 3 or 4 football pitches on the playing field which we also used for cricket during the summer. It was absolutely terrific because we would come straight out of the dormitory, they had elegant verandas at the end of the dormitories, and one would go straight out with a football or a bat and ball. For those of us who were sports minded it was a great opportunity. There was a great rivalry between the different dormitories. There were five different Houses, named after famous people in history; Wolfe, Drake (my house), Clive, Blake and Scott....I was captain of the football team.......

The school had its own allotments and there were two large stretches that were set aside on either side of the playing field for potatoes and probably other root vegetables (there was also an air raid shelter). One of our activities was certainly 'digging for victory' and it was trenching potatoes and we either did them at the school or went to surrounding farms. I can remember very well going behind a tractor and picking up the potatoes and putting them in a sack and we were paid 2d a sack. We also had our own pigs and chickens.

TEACHERS AS COOKS AND BOTTLE-WASHERS

Too Many Additional Tasks
During School Hours

NO PROSPECT OF WAR-TIME RELIEF

SOME OUTSPOKEN REMARKS WERE MADE BY MR. J. W. WARREN, TEACHERS' REPRESENTATIVE ON DORSET COUNTY EDUCATION COMMITTEE, AT A MEETING OF THE AUTHORITY ON MONDAY. HE ASSERTED THAT, TEACHERS WERE BECOMING HONORARY CLERKS TO THE TREASURY, HONORARY ASSISTANTS TO MILK PURVEYORS, HOUSEMAIDS, COOKS, AND BOTTLE WASHERS.

Mr. Warren was directing the attention of the committee to an administrative memorandum which referred to the anxiety of the Board of Education that teachers were being taken from their primary duty of teaching in order to attend to all sorts of things in school hours.

Dorset County Chronicle, 29th January 1942

As for teachers I think they must have done a good job. It must have been very difficult for them. They each had a very small room at the end of the dormitory.

Mrs Norman - the Headmaster's wife, showing boys at Kennylands how to darn socks

Of course in those days the cane was quite a common punishment and was quite normal. I can only remember going to the headmasters study once. You walked up the stairs with great trepidation and I duly asked for the cane and the book only to find to my great delight that the cane was broken, so I just reported back to my teacher and that was that....so I got away with it.

Great store was set about being self-sufficient and it was all a question of you making your own bed and darning your socks. Cleaning the dormitory was considered most important and I can remember on Saturdays it used to be, the floor used to be polished and a boy was pulled down on the carpet up and down whilst polishing the floor....Having to cope with living in that dormitory situation was pretty hard for some boys and they never did take to it, but I think I have thought in later years that during the war everything was abnormal, so abnormal became the normal, so I think for most of us we accepted it and grabbed the opportunity with both hands, certainly I did.

The situation we were in actually was a great leveller. With school uniforms for those of us who wouldn't have been able to afford things, as clothes were rationed, meant everybody was the same. We all wore patched up clothes. In fact we had a lady engaged just to patch and mend clothes, turning collars and cuffs, putting patches on elbows and knees on trousers.

We had a Scout troop formed towards the end of the war and we had a 'Gang Show'. We collected money for local charities.

As to our activities outside the camp I can remember there was a wood opposite called 'The Bird in the Hand Wood' where we used to have illegal fires and I can remember cooking potatoes and we had catapults which I am sure were not really permitted. We also went birds nesting which of course was very naughty, but not considered in such a bad light in those days....but certainly thinking it about it now I feel very guilty about doing it.

Another activity which was really a bit naughty was scrumping. Going for forays in the surrounding district and on another occasion I can remember we went to a house and there was a lady selling cherries from her tree and she suggested that we pick them ourselves, which of course was quite a fatal thing to do in our case and for our 3d or 6d I am afraid we got rather more than she would have expected us to.

On a more constructive side we did have the minister from the local church who used to come in and give services.......

I would say that the whole thing really was a great experience for us and something that I am very pleased to have gone through. It gave me an opportunity that I would never have had normally and on the education front it was probably better than we would have experienced in peace time'.

J.G. Suffolk

(Kennylands eventually closed in 1980)

SAYERS CROFT CAMP

'Our school, Catford Central Boys School, was very lucky. We were sent to a National Camps Corporation complex which was sited on Sayers Croft Farm at Ewhurst, Surrey. Here we were housed in cedarwood buildings, 40 boys and two masters in each of 5 dormitories. On the site were a craft block (with two masters), a block with classrooms, a hall, 'hospital block', staff quarters, dining hall etc. This presented our teachers with a problem; at Ashford (where the school had been evacuated to before Sayers Camp) they only had to look after us during school hours and church parade, now they had our charge for 24 hours a day, seven days a week. It was resolved after a Rota system was developed and it worked very well.

The five dormitories were each named after Castles and conveniently gave us rival teams for games and other activities. We were allocated small plots to grow our own produce. Parties were sent to local farms to assist in planting and harvesting potatoes etc. I recall on one occasion after planting a row of cabbages we were given permission to use a private swimming pool. Not having any costumes we stripped and dived in not realising that we were in full view from a local hill!

Whortle berries, when in season, were collected from this local hill for use in the kitchen. Foxgloves were collected and sent to be processed to extract Digitalis.

Parents day was once a month and those who were able to came by coach to be met in the village. I remember taking my parents to see a crater made by a stray bomb near the village only to be told that there was one like that in their back garden in London. (A young girl was killed in the Anderson shelter in the garden but fortunately my mother had just gone to the shops when it fell otherwise she would probably have been killed. They then had to be housed in requisitioned property till after the war.) Often we saw vapour trails and dogfights overhead during the Battle of Britain. On one occasion a few incendiary bombs fell in the camp and were dealt with by a master stealthily approaching, protected by a dustbin lid!

Out of school activities needed to be organised and we played cricket, stoolball, rounders and football. If the weather was bad we played board games, whist, 'beetle drives', table tennis etc. in the hall. From time to time we had film shows. Before one of the masters, Harry Gell, was called up to serve in the tank regiment, he helped us to put on concerts and the boys made the costumes and props from whatever came to hand. I recall performing a couple of comic songs of which my father still had the music from his time in the First World War.

Before I left school at Easter 1942, aged 15, I was chosen to do a project by the art master, Arthur Evens. This was to be a design for a mural that was later to be painted in oils in the dining hall. Another lad was chosen to do a design portraying 'summer' activities and mine was to cover 'winter'. With a lot of help from the Art master I managed to complete my design but left school before there was time to do the enlarged oils. I was invited back for the unveiling, the finished version having been completed by two younger boys. Fortunately I was able to keep the original design which I still treasure.

Len Davies at Sayers Croft Camp with the 'Winter' mural and original design

The days at Sayers Camp were indeed a very happy and special never-to-be-forgotten part of my life.

Over the years my thoughts have often wandered back to those halcyon days of the early part of the war and a few years ago I took my wife back to see if Sayers Camp was still there. It had survived and happily is thriving as a Field Centre for educational purposes. I was highly delighted to find the camp almost unchanged from all those years ago. The trees we planted were now very much bigger, and one of the air-raid shelters is still there. A solar-heated swimming pool has been added and also a sports building in similar style to the old cedar units. Dormitories have been modified inside to conform with modern ideas and have been made much more comfortable. In the dining hall the two murals remain as a reminder of those long gone days'.

(One of the masters, Harry Gell, died in November 1997, but 50 of the old school boys subscribed to a bronze plaque dedicated to him for his educational connections with the camp throughout his life. It is in the dining hall of the present Sayers Croft Field Centre and was unveiled by the Mayor of Lewisham. It has since been registered as a War Memorial.)

L.D. Welling

Len Davies' mother at Sayers Croft Camp, 1940

Bill Davies, Catford Central Old Boy at Sayers Croft Camp, 1994
This photo was taken from the same place as the one in 1940
There are remarkably few changes

THE WARREN FARM, LEWKNOR, OXFORDSHIRE

B. Balding (top, 4th from left) with teachers at Warren Farm
(Music teacher Miss Lynn is the woman on the right)

'The house was a big double-fronted house with a lawn in front. To the left of the house there was a concrete path leading to two or three steps. Up these you then stood on a patio. Three steps forward you reached a door and on opening this you stepped into a dormitory holding about 20 beds. This was to be my home for the next 15 months.

It was owned by Sir Edward Cadogan who was on the board of Governors of Eton College. This place was a sort of summer camp for the lads who did not go home in the summer.....

The little estate consisted of the big house, dormitory, Dutch barn with three indoor tennis courts, two outside tennis courts, full size outdoor swimming pool, cricket pitch, rugby pitch and a cricket pavilion which, in our time there, doubled as a school room during the week and a Church on Sundays.

To the right of the house there were miles of woods and Beech trees which were to be our playground.

That same day we were sorted out. There were about 20 lads of mixed ages. Me and about three others were the eldest. We had two teachers one male and one female called Miss Lynn, the school's music teacher, and about three female helpers who cooked and fed us better than others. We in turn were expected to look after the dormitory, make our beds, keep ourselves clean, these three tasks had mixed results. It was just like being a boarding school....

Helpers outside the dormitory at Warren Farm
(B. Balding's mother is on the right)

Our routine was soon established. School was held daily in the cricket pavilion which as I said turned into a Church on Sunday with a visiting Jesuit priest coming from Oxford each week. He had a duty to say about six masses each Sunday morning. We were his altar boys. The Mass was slightly different to what we were used to . A normal mass takes about half an hour, his took about 6-8 minutes all said in Latin. He most definitely was a man in a hurry. We thought the world of him because we had a quick Mass and then back into the woods to play.

The school was kept up in the pavilion for as long as possible, but with winter coming on it became the job of us elder lads to go out and get wood as various fires had to be kept going, the pavilion, the big house and for cooking.....

As winter progressed more wood was required and schooling for us went out of the window. The snow came so thick that we could not get to the pavilion so school was held in the Dormitory but it was cold. Remember there were no long trousers in those days, so legs became chapped red raw where short trousers rubbed in one place and wellington boots in another.

Recreation came in many forms. Our main meeting place was our dormitory. At night we lay in bed and the elder kids would tell stories about ghosts. When he stayed, Sir Edward always came into our dormitory and gave us sweets from a great big jar.

We roamed the woods. We all had our secret trails and hideouts.

During the winter our school decided to put on a show for local people so our 'Minstrel' concert was born.

Another bright idea was that us older lads should go to the main school in Chinnor and do woodwork. We walked the 2-3 miles on Friday afternoons. The local yokels found out and they started to waylay us with slug guns, catapults, home made bows and arrows...we had the lot. We respond and there is trouble all around, caused mainly by 'the 'vaccies' so we were told. PC Plod sorted us all out. Still I did make a very nice stool for my mum'.

B.B. Romford

'We found ourselves moved to a third and last location where we stayed for the remainder of our three-year exile. Our new home was a spartan, army-type Nissen hut, once an isolation hostel for patients with infectious diseases. The building was off by itself in a field, bordering on a lonely, windswept moor, about a mile out of the village. There were about a

dozen evacuees at this lonely outpost supervised by two women from our hometown (Tyneside).

It was a regimental existence. We slept in a dormitory, heated by a pot-bellied stove, and ate our meals from a bare, wooden table. It was not unusual to see earwigs scurrying across the table.

I can still picture us all chorusing the inevitable postscript after every meal 'Thank God for a good dinner. May we leave the table please?'

Still, our new billet offered a spacious playground with much to explore. We discovered an unused army pill-box lookout station on the moor which we put to imaginative use.

We were still living at the hostel when my father died on Remembrance Day 1942. Such stunning news was given to us at school by the headmaster. Shortly after this, my mother came to take us home for good. Mixed with the sadness of my father's death was the enormous sense of freedom I felt at being liberated from my evacuation'.

M.K. Ontario

parental visits

Some billets were in such isolated communities that parental visits were difficult to arrange, as the following two extracts, from evacuees billeted in the same place, illustrate.

'My mother was not able to visit Feckenham very often, public transport only brought Mum from Birmingham to Astwood Bank, and a two mile walk in all weathers made it a long and slow journey. Each visit, about every six to eight weeks was awaited with eager anticipation bringing sweets, cakes and a little pocket money. Each visit passed all too quickly ending in sadness'.

B.F. Sutton Coldfield

'Visits from my parents were probably at monthly intervals as the only day that they could travel to Feckenham would have been a Sunday. Most people worked till midday on Saturday and the journey by bus was far too long for a Saturday afternoon. In fact the bus on a Sunday only went as far as Astwood Bank and the rest of the next 2-3 miles were on foot. I well remember my mother coming on her own on one occasion and having a lift with the local Doctor. She vowed never to get in the car again as he thought he was on a race track not a country lane'.

H.S.

'Although neither my sister nor I went back to Dover during the four years or so of evacuation, my parents managed about two visits a year, my father coming at Easter and my mother in the summer. Their journeys by train, standing all the way in the blackout, must have been something of an ordeal and fraught with some danger as on one occasion the train was attacked by enemy aircraft. I remember being acutely embarrassed by my father's South London/Kentish accent which sounded so odd among the Welsh accents to which I had become accustomed. I think that my parents were probably glad to get back to each other in Dover, where they seemed to find life more exciting than dangerous. Oddly enough, I

was always more upset when my father went back than when my mother did. During their stay in Wales it was arranged for Mary and me to be with them throughout their visit, which entailed some re-arranging of sleeping accommodation in both families'.

M.E. Haverfordwest

Visits To Evacuation Areas

FURTHER railway trips at special cheap fares for relatives and friends to visit evacuees in West-Country reception areas have been arranged for February 25 and March 3. It was found possible, in connection with the January trips, to provide special 'bus services to a large number of villages to which normally there is no 'bus service. These arrangements will again be made.

On February 25 a train from Paddington will run to Bridport, Dorchester. Maiden Newton and Weymouth, whil a train from Waterloo on the same day will serve, among other places, Gillingham, Sherborne, Stalbridge, and Sturminster Newton.

Corfe Cast, Poole, Swanage and Wareham car be visited by relatives of evacuees on March 3, a special train being run from Waterloo.

Dorset Daily Echo, 15th February 1940

Some parents had problems visiting their children for other reasons....

'Thurs.

My Dear Benny,

I suppose you will be wondering why I am writing again, but when Mrs Colenutt went to Greenwich to get the vouchers, the man told her that the coaches are arranged for the 23rd not the 30th, that date being the last Sunday in the month which should be Parents Day.

Mrs Colenutt argued and said it has always been the last Sunday in the month but the man said the 23rd, and he asked Mrs Colenutt if she knew anyone who was going to the camp to tell them the date. But we want to know if Mr Wille knows, so will you find out and let me know as soon as possible if the 23rd is correct. If so Maurice had better write to his Mum and tell her because she will think it will be the last Sunday and I don't suppose Mr Wille will have two Parents Days in a month. I am sending you a stamped envelope, so Cheerio for now.

With Love....'

B.E. Bexleyheath

For one particular evacuee the visit of her mother was to have unfortunate results...

'I had settled down well in my billet until my mother came.....Once she had met my mother, my friend was cool to me because she realised that I was from a different class. My foster mother told me that the parents of my friend were paying extra for her keep so I was not to be too disappointed if she received more treats than I did. I think that was the worst thing that had ever happened to me'.

E.G. (no address)

overseas

CHILD EVACUEES TO AMERICA

SECRETARY'S APPEAL TO RHODES SCHOLARS

Swarthmore, Pennsylvania,
Monday.

Mr. Frank Aydelotte, American secretary of the Rhodes Scholarships, has appealed to American Rhodes scholars throughout the United States to help in plans to house British children in the United States for the duration of the war.

He suggests that they should receive into their families one or more children "of Oxford and Cambridge dons or children of other British universities.'

Plans to provide homes for 200 British children are being drawn up at Mobile, Alabama, by the advisory board of the Salvation Army.—Reuter.

Dorset Daily Echo, 1st July 1940

The following extracts are from an important historical document and I am indebted to Margaret Wood, herself an evacuee on the Llanstephan Castle to South Africa, who has provided extracts from the diary of 'M.P.Richardson' who went to South Africa on the same ship. Every effort has been made to trace the diarist so if he, she, or anyone else, recognises the name or the contents would they please contact the publishers. Some of the writing is now unclear and I apologise for any mistakes in transcription.

'Diary of Journey to South Africa. 1940
August 19th Monday

Left Brentwood on the train with Ben, Pam, Kay, Bill, Ronald, Bruce.....in company of Miss Townshend escort. Went to Liverpool. Travelled to

Euston. Had a special train to Liverpool. Went to Childwall Valley High School (*) by special bus. Had supper. Went to bed. 3 Blankets and no pillow.

(*) Childwall Valley School no longer exists and is now the site of a housing estate in Liverpool. However, it was a girls school during the war years which would suggest that the diarist is female.

August 20 Tuesday

Miss Turner left us and Miss Nunham took her place.

August 21 Wednesday

Had our luggage checked. Were given coloured section tapes. (Pink and Green)

August 22 Thursday

Had a concert. Beryl, Jose and I did a sketch. Mrs Waterson, wife of the High Commissioner for S.A. came to see us, also Geoffrey Shakespeare, MP for the Scilly Isles and ....who laid the foundation stone of the school and the Mayor of Liverpool came. I got several peoples autographs.

August 23 Friday

Went to the docks at 12. Boarded the Llanstephan Castle at half-past two. Had dinner then Boat Drill. We moved to the mouth of the river at 6.30. Lights out at 9.00pm.

August 24 Saturday

Had boat drill. Inspected by man from the Board of Trade.

RULES.
Rise 7.15 am
On Deck 7.45
Breakfast 8.00
Dinner 12.30
Rest 2.30 - 4.00
Tea 5.30

During rest hours we started sailing. At 4.30 Barber's shop opened. We bought sweets. 30 ships joined us. Passed the Cumberland coast at 7pm.

August 25 Sunday

Sighted Ireland and Scotland. Had a service at 11.am in 1st Class lounge. Beryl, Jean, Jose and I were sea-sick.

August 26 Monday

Everyone felt ill. I was sea sick. I had no meal until tea-time. Shirley was sick 8 times.

August 27 Tuesday

All felt much better. Weren't allowed to have sweets until we had 3 meals. We have travelled 1000 miles North and are now travelling West.

August 28 Wednesday

Convoy left us in the night. Had a lecture on African religion and a lecture on Music. We saw a school of porpoises.

August 29 Thursday

9.30 Medical parade.

10.15 Boat Drill.

10.30 Religious Instruction.

11.30 Lecture on South Africa. Capetown.

6.00 Concert.

August 30 Friday

Had a lesson in Afrikaans. At 4.15 we had a Treasure Hunt.

August 31 Saturday

Miss Durham treated us to drinks. Did our mending. Had a lecture from Doctor Sherring. Had a party from 8 - 10.30pm.

September 1 Sunday

Had a service taken by the Captain. The Officers have changed into white uniform. 2.00- 4.00 we ran into a tropical storm which lasted 4 minutes.

September 2 Monday

Saw some flying fish.

September 3 Tuesday

Had congregational instruction from Mr Evans (much better). 4-15 we had a Treasure Hunt.

September 4 Wednesday

Lecture from Dr. Low on his tour of Canada & USA. Had a Whist Drive. Highest score 115. Jose got 103.

Saw some flying fish.

September 5 Thursday

Got up at 6.am and went on deck and saw flying fishes.

September 6 Friday

Saw some sharks. Were given Quinine Tablets. Played Deck Quoits.

September 9 Saturday

Saw lots of porpoises. Saw the first ship for 11 days at 10.30. Had a talk on the ship by Mr Campbell, 4th Officer. At 12 we sighted Freetown. Saw a whale. We stopped in the Harbour at about 2pm. Saw several natives come in canoes to try and sell their goods. At dusk we had to dress in pyjama suits to keep away the mosquitoes. Had a concert.

September 8 Sunday

Some native canoes came. Some exchanged their goods, some sang and some dived for coins. The country looks much nicer than England.

September 9 Monday

An oil tanker came alongside with a Chinese crew. We left Freetown during the tea-time.

September 10 Tuesday

We all decided to put Miss Durham in Coventry because of the ironing. Had Deck Games.

September 11 Wednesday

4.30 pm we were shown over the Bridge by Mr. Harvey, 2nd Officer. We crossed the equator during tea. Had a Whist Drive and I came 3rd.

September 12 Thursday

Had boat drill on boat deck.

September 13 Friday

Had a lark in the night. Rosemary and I changed beds and twisted Mr. Brown (1st tourist Steward.)

September 14 Saturday

Had a good concert given by the Escorts. Jack bagged us half-a pound of biscuits for a feast on Monday.

September 15 Sunday

Service at 11.30 given by the Captain. Mr Harvey, 2nd Officer, sat with us for dinner. Jack bagged us a tin sardines, pkt. of biscuits and 12 chocolate biscuits.

September 16 Monday

10.30pm. Jack came in with a plate of cake and bread. We had 3 sardines on bread, 2 pieces of cake and 4 biscuits.

September 17 Tuesday

Had our photos. taken with the captain.

September 18 Wednesday

Had boat Drill.

September 19 Thursday

Packed our cases ready to disembark on Friday.

September 20 Friday

Disembarked. Paper reporters took our photos. Went to 'Westbrook', Sir Patrick Duncan's house. Had tea. Went to a Jewish Orphanage.

September 21 Saturday

Went to a garden party at 'Westbrook' in the afternoon. Met an old school girl.

September 22 Sunday

Went to Capetown Cathedral in the morning. Went to Muirzenberg in the afternoon.

September 23 Monday

Went shopping and to Cape Town Museum in the morning.

September 24 Tuesday

Went to Camps Bay for a picnic with Mrs Daysch. Went to Cape Town swimming baths.

September 25 Wednesday

Went swimming at Muirzenberg.

September 26 Thursday

Went to see Rhodes Memorial.

September 27 Friday

Nothing happened.

U.S. WANT CHILDREN OF ALL CLASSES

CITIES REQUEST "SEND ALL YOU CAN"

Dorset Daily Echo, 6th July 1940

problems & concerns

Not all evacuees had a good time, or were well treated in their billets. The following are just a few examples.

'We were told to stay out of the house during the day and only return at meal times, which were sparse and frugal. In fact we were so hungry we would collect apples that had fallen from the trees and were beginning to rot. On one occasion my mother told us to smuggle some of the apples into the house, hiding them in our knickers. On climbing the stairs the elastic in my knickers snapped and the apples went bouncing down the stairs. The hosts called us 'English Thieves' and threw the apples into the waste bin.....

The hosts and other locals constantly told us that Liverpool was being heavily bombed and the city had been flattened. Although at the time we did not know, Liverpool was bombed in 1940.

English news was not allowed on the radio, therefore the news was always in Welsh so we never knew what was happening regarding the war and the outside world. This caused confusion and tremendous concern for the evacuees, who were obviously concerned about their relatives and friends back home in Liverpool. English was never spoken in our presence except to give reprimands and scare mongering'.

L.G. Warrington

'I was evacuated to Ironbridge until I was 9-10 years old. The people I stayed with wanted to adopt me as they had no children. My mother had a hard time getting me back. They sent me to a Protestant School and changed my name. They gave my mother a hard time sending Health Visitors to her home to check out the house and the other children.

I remember that she had to go to court to get me back. I also remember the Priest coming to see me and telling them I had to go to a Catholic School. Every time my mother came to see me they would make some excuse as to why she couldn't. After a while I was frightened of her....

One day I was in school when the Evacuation Officer came to collect me with my Mother and Aunt telling me they were taking me for new clothes to town. We went to the Railway Station. I knew I was going back. I don't know how, or if, the poor man survived as I had my two arms tight around his neck. They managed to get me on the train in the end. Once I was home and had met my family I calmed down....'

S.J. Liverpool

'Joseph was a very quiet boy. He was placed in a house whose garden backed onto the one I was in. After Mum had gone back home his torment started. The woman was the local 'fallen woman'. He was not allowed to stay in the house when she was out. She drank and used to vent her wrath on my brother. He was hit and starved, one meal a day if he was lucky. He would come to the fence at the bottom of the garden and I would save him some of my food and pass it over. When the lady of my house found out she made him a bag of food up each day.

When the time came for us to move to the farm my host told my Dad when he came to see us that Joseph should be taken home because she was worried that he would suffer even more. Never at any time during our evacuation that I can remember did any official body visit to see how we were faring. Nobody cared. Joseph went home and then got a placement in North Wales. Dad brought him to visit me at the farm before he went to Wales. Our Mum wrote our addresses down for him and told him to keep it safe in case he needed to write to me.

I later got a dirty piece of notepaper, on it was written 'HELP ME' Joseph. This I passed on to my father the next time he visited. I never saw Joseph for 4 years after that, but later I learnt that my father had gone to Wales the next day and found my brother with a harness on him tied to a cart which had tree trunks on it.....He took Joseph home with him that day and that was a huge relief to me. He did not go away again and when I finally came home we were like strangers, as was all of my family, we never had the closeness of a family that we had had before the war'.

Doreen was billeted next door but one to Joseph. She was 10 and trying to be mother to us all but she had an awful time. I remember going out to the back garden and saw her shouting at Joseph, then she waved at me, the next thing the woman came out of her house, wrapped Doreen's hair around her fingers and dragged her back into the house by her hair. She was told not to speak to us again and we used to meet in secret by the swings'.

R.C. Birkenhead

'We were evacuated from Birkenhead to B.C. We arrived at the home of a woman and her elderly father....The following day we were given a set of house rules:

> *We must never go beyond the downstairs back living room, only go up stairs to bed, when we must be accompanied at all times.*
>
> *Never to answer a ring at the front door.*

The cottage had two rooms downstairs and two bedrooms....we had to share the one bedroom with Miss. and her double bed. On the bed lay a long rope and this caused us great fear as I thought she was going to hit us with it. Miss. then told us that we would be tied to the bed so she would know if we got out and wandered about, because the rope would be loose......

We had very little food as we were constantly reminded that there was a war on, but we did get cheese rind with bits of cheese on it.

Miss. refused to have my sister home during the day and as she had only just turned 4 years, was not allowed to be registered at the local school, but as a small concession was allowed to sit on a small chair outside my classroom during school hours.

When some local boys found out where we were staying they kept asking me why young women went to the cottage at night....One night I plucked up the courage to ask the old man about the young women coming to the cottage. He looked quite shocked and told me never to mention the subject again or I would get into a lot of trouble with his daughter.

One evening Miss went out leaving us in with her father. Normally we were sent out to play but my sister had a bad throat so we were allowed to stay in. The door bell rang and Mr. told me to answer the door and show the person into the front room. When I opened the door there was a young lady there distressed and crying. I unlocked the front room and took her in. I was shocked as I expected it to be a parlour but found it looked like a hospital room. A bed with a white sheet on and lots of instruments and glass jars on a trolley.

Mr. told me to go back into the other room and never tell his daughter what had happened or there would be big trouble...

I was told by the children we played with that Miss had had some boys before us but they left because of her cruel treatment.

Lots of questions remained unanswered:-

1.   Why were we allowed to go to a house that had no bed for us, leaving us to share a bed with a strange woman?

2.   Why was my sister allowed to sit all day in a school corridor without books, toys etc.?

3.   Why didn't any official check us out to see if we were being well looked after?'

P.P. Birkenhead

'I was evacuated when I was going on 4 years old. I had a terrible time that it took until my late twenties before I came to terms with it. I had blocked most of it out and it came back in parts when I was 10-11 years old and then I blacked out or had screaming fits, that's when I looked at my arms and hands and body it was small. I was back to 4 years old and living it.

The outline was I was put in a dog kennel with a collar and chain round my neck and locked up in the kennel at night and the dog was put in my bed with four other children, including my sister, 6 years old. I fretted for my Mum and I wet the bed so that was my punishment. I can still hear her steps coming up the stairs to feel the bed when we were all in it to see if I wet it. She carried the chain and collar with her, put the chain and collar on and then took me down crying for my Mum. Then she chained me to the kennel where I stayed till the following morning, when they all got up. It was winter and cold and my cries would also echo around the kennel. It sounded hollow and I had more nightmares than ever'.

B.W. Bootle

'My two brothers and I were evacuated from East Ham two days before the 2nd World War, September 1939. The school I attended was Monega Rd. Junior School in East Ham. We were evacuated to a village of Stalham in Norfolk. All three of us were billeted with three families for different periods of time. Two of the families were very good but one couple treated us very badly. We were allowed on Christmas morning to play with the presents our parents had sent us and then told to go out and play in the snow....we never saw our presents again.

We also had to stay in a garden shed and only allowed in the house to go to bed from November 1939-March 1940, and we had to break the ice in the water butt to have a wash.'

A.F.J.G.

(Evacuated later to Bagnall.) When we arrived in Bagnall my younger brother and I were billeted with one family and my middle brother with another.

'One day we were in the village. We had a 6d Postal Order and had bought some little loaves. We were standing eating them when we saw my Mum walking towards us. She had come to visit and was shocked at the way we were eating the bread. We were taken back to the billet and my mother saw that we were washed and clothed and told the woman what she thought of her, got the clothes she could and took us home. My brother had blond hair and you could see the lice in it'.

M.A.W. Liverpool

'My mother took me to the village of C. When she left I was taken upstairs and showed where I was to sleep. The bed was a wooden frame and the middle was sacking tacked on with little tacks. I spent most of my nights banging tacks back in with my shoe.

.....The four of us in the house were made to sit with our hands on our heads for hours and we were beaten regularly with a stick that always stood in the fire-place.

I was left alone at first but I remember the boys were made to walk around the room with their penises on plates. I know they slept in the woman's bed every night in turn. All of a sudden a man appeared in the house. I was told years later that he was a deserter from the Army. That's when my abuse started. I was never raped but every night he would wake me up and stand over me. He would then take my hand and place it on his penis. I would turn away and he would go around the other side of the bed and do the same again. This went on for ever.....

Eventually the police came to get him.

E.J. Liverpool

'.....I tried to stop the lady beating the dog. She let it go and told me to put my hand out and I thought she was going to hit me with her cane, but she pulled the poker from the fire and put it across my hand'.

E.J. Liverpool

'I was evacuated to near Stroud. Had two ghastly spinster women who cared for us. They were a sadistic couple. Froze in winter. We never had gloves, cardigans or wellies when there was thick snow, consequently chilblains would crack and burst on our hands and feet and the backs of our legs were red raw. My neck would ache with hunching up with the cold. To this day I put heating on before anything else. We would only be given a blanket so we'd wrap our own feet in our night gowns and crunch up, but would wake up when we stretched our legs and hit the cold sheets....Though we were not starved, we were pretty near the border line. I recall being woken up with the gnawing pangs of hunger which overcame my fear of raiding the larder in the early hours of the morning. So in the dark I spread thick marg. on a slice of bread and crept back to bed with my booty. I took a big bite and swallowed Ugh! I had spread it thickly with lard. I was so sick but had to finish it up as I couldn't afford to leave the evidence. I remember during the hot summers, we did have them then, we would be so thirsty, we were not allowed any water, so we'd drink from the outside loos.

At one time I was so driven to despair that I attempted to cut my throat. I was 10 years old....the knife was blunt.

H. London

Borough of Marlborough

BOROUGH ACCOUNTANT
TEL. No 118.

W. H. VOWLES.
TOWN CLERK.

Council Offices,
Marlborough, Wilts.

28th Sept. 1940.

Dear Sir,

London Evacuation.

Referring to your letter of the 27th instant. Since the arrival of evacuees from Bexhill we are being continually asked to provide accommodation for stragglers from London. The provision of this has entailed the use of all Condemned Houses and the point has been reached when no further accommodation is available.

At the moment we have four mothers and babies in the Rest Room waiting for billets.

Under these circumstances I am bound to say that we cannot take any more.

Yours faithfully,

W. H. Vowles

Town Clerk.

P.A.Selbourne Stringer, Esq.,
Clerks Office,
County Offices,
TROWBRIDGE,
Wilts.

This letter illustrates the pressures on Town Clerks to find extra billets (There were particular problems in Wiltshire because of the number of temporary Army camps in the area)

This evacuee and her twin brother were 7 at the time these events took place. The third of four evacuations.

'Evacuated again to Whitminster to live with our Grandparent's next door neighbour. No big sister this time to look after us. The neighbours had three sons. The eldest one was a few years older than us. He had some friends and the nightmare began. In the field adjoining the foster parents back garden he and his friends would gang up on us.

First of all they made me lay down in he field on my back with my arms and legs spread out. They took it in turns to put twigs into my vagina, forcing my twin brother to stand and watch. Then I had to stand up and my twin made to bend over forward behind me and hold my hands with his hands and one of the boys would jump onto my brother's back and we had to let them trot around the field horse and cart style giving them a ride, then we had to reverse our positions. This went on until all the boys had had their ride.

We were often chased across field and pushed into cow pats.

Every Sunday lunchtime the foster father would stand at the meal table and swing his leather belt in front of us and ask which one of us wanted it first for a good thrashing..although he never actually hit us. All these things happened on a regular basis for a 'bit of fun' and looking back I wonder who the enemy really was....

My twin and I never had anyone to talk to during our stay in Whitminster. We seem to have been struck dumb, we still are to a certain extent over the abuse and cruelty, we never talk about it as it is nothing to be proud of. I did try talking to my foster father about the leather belt and the cow pats incidents and his reply was 'Oh that! That was just a bit of fun'. I rest my case. Us evacuees were just a 'bit of fun' to a lot of people who were supposed to be looking after us'.

A.D. Gravesend

This letter provides a rare insight into the fears many evacuees must have been harbouring throughout their evacuation and which were rarely considered by those looking after their welfare.

'When the issue of my second evacuation came up, I can recall that my main fear of being separated from my mother and father was that they would be killed and I would become an orphan. This was not a consideration when I went to Dorchester (1st Evacuation), but seemed all too real by October 1940. It was not so much the demise of my parents itself that was uppermost in my mind, but what I thought was the inevitable consequence of becoming an orphan, that of having to live in an orphanage. Based only on hearsay, and perhaps 'Oliver Twist' I had a basic dread of such establishments. I made my parents promise that they would always go into the Anderson shelter as soon as the night sirens sounded'.

A.K. Nottingham

EVACUEES—PLEASANT AND OTHERWISE

Sir John Lorden, of Eastbourne, a former M.P., referring to the billeting of evacuees at the annual meeting of the National Federation of Property Owners in London today, said: "I am not objecting to it. But some people have come along and practically destroyed properties, making them in a terrible mess, and trouble has ensued.

"In some cases most pleasant people have come. You could not wish for better. But some children brought to our neighbourhood are not nice to have in your house. They have brought into them livestock, which we had not had before. It is a very serious matter for property owners."

Dorset Daily Echo, 25th January 1940

THE return home

'I returned to London in July 1942 when I left school to find employment. I hate London as it was then, all the shops boarded up. It was not the London I had known. I worked as a Post Office Telephonist which I enjoyed. Raids were still going on at this time and I was in a bombing incident at the Kennington Oval.....I got a transfer in the Post Office to Shaftesbury. I lodged with my (evacuee) foster parents in Sturminster Newton and used to cycle to Shaftesbury to work. In the winter I lodged at Shaftesbury with some friends'.

S.R. Gillingham, Dorset

'Weston was bombed again and again.....My mother and father decided we should go back home to London - why not all die together!? But by now I did not want to go home. Weston was my home now. The family were so kind to me. I loved the sea, I loved walking over the causeway to Anchor Head, and Kewstoke Woods I adored. I cried and cried. I felt I shouldn't be feeling like this but I wanted so much to stay at Weston. I remember passing the bungalow on my way back to London. I leaned out of the window and waved and they waved back. I sobbed and sobbed........How I missed everything when I got home and my brother did too. We both wanted to stay in Weston so much. I felt guilty, I felt that I shouldn't be feeling like this....

I still go back to Weston...in a way it is still my home...'

L.M. Southgate

'I was enjoying myself as an evacuee. I was coming home late in the evenings as I was dating a couple of Radcliffe girls. After six weeks of this pleasant life my hostess, whom I'm sure didn't really want me in the first place, gave me ten shillings and my ration book and told me to go home. So off I went with my suitcase to Nottingham where I caught the train to London and then travelled to Southall by Tube and bus. My parents were somewhat surprised to see me........Later my father received a letter from my hostess asking for the ten shillings she had given me to get home. I *have often wondered what he said in his reply. I don't think it was very polite and he didn't send any money'.*

C.H. Tylers Green

'The most difficult part of being evacuated is coming home again. It was the worst day of my whole life. When the time came I had completely forgotten my family and London. I was ten years old and suddenly I was to be taken away by this strange lady called Mother, from all these wonderful people I had grown up with and not only from them but the whole village that I knew and loved. I knew every path, track and lane for miles around, every house and cottage, every man, woman and child, every cat, dog, cow and chicken. It was lovely, beautiful world and I had to leave it all behind'.

P.R. Maidstone

'I went home such a different child. I didn't seem to fit in so well. My sister hated my country accent and I found that everything was so different as I had been away four years'.

M.H. Bristol

'I personally had become very attached to the little Devon village I had 'grown up' in and I had made friends with a local girl, we still correspond. I did not want to go back to London. My parents had moved to another district and I did not want the upheaval. Nevertheless I returned, but somehow the closeness of family never really returned. My family was in Devon in my billet'.

J.H. Kent

'One morning I was helping Mrs Cudd to shell peas and she was crying. I had never seen her cry before. Her tears were dripping into the peas, I remember that clearly. She told me that my mother was coming that day to take me back to London. I was bewildered. I had been with Mrs Cudd for four years and as far as I knew SHE was my mother. It was awful when my mother arrived. Mrs Cudd tried to persuade my mother to let her adopt me. I suppose it was a very tense time for them both.

As we walked away down the lane the sight of Mrs Cudd wiping her eyes on her apron was too much for me. I was only six years old and I screamed after her 'I want my mummy'. To me she was my mummy.

I often wonder what kind of life I would have had if Mrs Cudd had been allowed to adopt me, because the life I had with my real parents was one of physical and sexual abuse and to this day I am still suffering from the effects'.

A.D. Romford

'Time to leave our foster parents. The war was now close to an end. Excitement for us going home but I must relate I cannot recall how my foster parents must have felt. They obviously loved us and it must have left a huge gap in their lives....

Liverpool, home to a city and strange new life. Back again to square one, this time in reverse. I spoke with a strong Welsh lilt so once again I had to 'run the gauntlet'.....I can recall that I found my new life even harder to adjust to. My father and mother were virtually strangers and to this very day I found or thought something in my life was missing, like a piece of jigsaw, and I could never find it'.

P.B. Liverpool

'I count myself very, very lucky to have been brought up by such a loving, caring couple, Mammie and Jack. I lived with them for 5 years (from 3.5 to 8.5 years of age) and it broke my heart to leave them, and the friends that I made. It was the only life that I knew. I could speak and understand Welsh, I felt Welsh and to me, it felt as though I was leaving home. Although I was going back home to England to live with Mum and Dad and my brother and sister, I'm sure that the situation didn't really make me as happy as it should have done. I was going to live in a completely different world, and I didn't know what to expect. It took my sister and I a long, long time to settle down with Mum and Dad, my brother had already returned home quite a while before us, so he was fine. All we wanted to do was to go back to be with our Welsh families so Mum and Dad arranged for us to spend our long school summer holidays with them each year. My sister and I used to speak Welsh to each other at home sometimes and, as

you can imagine, it used to annoy Mum and Dad and we would get a telling off'.

J.H. Upminster

'War came to an end while we were evacuated in Darlington, Co. Durham. There were street parties to celebrate. Tom and I were not allowed to attend because we 'did not belong up North!'. We did catch their fleas though and brought them back with us to Gravesend, much to the disgust of our mother. Out came the black double-edged tooth comb and some nasty smelling flea treatment. Our heads bent over a newspaper with mother scraping the comb through our heads. Gravesend too had celebration street parties but we were not allowed to attend these either because we had been evacuated to safety....some safety!! We didn't seem to belong anywhere. Our accents were a combination of Gloucestershire, Darlington and Gravesend...and we took some teasing over that too'.

unusual events

'My sister and I were sent to Boxford in Berkshire....when I look back at the air-raid precautions that were taken it was laughable. If there was a warning the local vicar used to cycle round the village ringing a handbell!'

D.L. Romford

'Leaving Chapel one Sunday we walked into an air-raid casualty exercise on the village square. We were ordered to be casualties by some man in a uniform, bandaged up and put into a makeshift ambulance. This ended up at Redditch Hospital, 5 miles away! We were unloaded and told we could go home. So we said 'Yes, but how? It's Sunday ..no buses!' Some kind person said that they would run us back. We ended up being late for Sunday dinner'.

R.B.

(Evacuee from Edinburgh to North Berwick)

'.....George (brother) and I were moved to an Hotel which had been requisitioned to house Evacuees. After a few months all the inmates were moved to a place called Christie Homes, I think it might have been similar to Barnardos, and stayed there until a Mine, which had broken loose from a string across the Firth of Forth, blew up outside the Home breaking all the windows'.

C. J. Aukland, New Zealand

'My hostess was somewhat limited. Her main hobby was making the most perfect spills out of old newspapers for lighting the fire. I was present when a friend arrived with her Christmas present, a book. She handed it back unopened saying 'No thanks! We've already got a book'.

D.T. Reading

work

(See also the section on Camp Schools)

Some evacuees were given paid work to do or volunteered to do farm labouring and other tasks to supplement their income. Potato picking was particularly popular...

> '.....in the early winter of 1941, I think it was November, we were asked to go potato picking. With pound signs in my eyes and visions of having wealth beyond belief, I went potato picking for a fortnight, half days only, earning the princely sum of 2/6d. Needless to say I was disappointed. With the money I earned I bought a gun and holster, for our games of 'Cowboys and Indians...'
>
> **D.P.**

> 'The local farmers used the older boys for potato picking and mangel-wurzel cutting. A blue card was issued from the Education Authority, marked in 40 half-day squares which the farmer had to sign when we'd completed half a day and we were allowed time off from school to work twenty days each year for a farmer of our choice. The pay was 5 shillings a day and as many potatoes as you could carry'.
>
> **G.B.** Kent

> 'Sometimes, during the summer, along with other children from the area, we would help with the potato picking and fruit harvesting which we were paid for. We then took it in turns to ride home on the Shire Horses'.
>
> **M.P.** South Wirral

AND PEAS!

> 'There was at this time, a shortage of labour for harvesting and I went out one day to pick peas for 1/- or so a basket. In the event I earned nothing as I didn't fill the basket and I ate more than I put in the basket. I still love eating raw peas'.
>
> **C.H.** Tylers Green

'Come the summer very often our labour was volunteered. I say this because I can't remember anyone offering to go and work in the fields picking things, peas, cabbage. We pulled, picked all these things. No one ever paid us. We got it in kind, a bag of peas, or cabbage from the family we were hired out to.

Another job was working for the stud at Aston Rowant. We cleaned the stables, in fact we did everything that they wanted us to do and for my part I enjoyed it. We worked very hard in these stables and one day the lady asked me if there was anything I would like and I asked if I could ride a horse. She said no but would walk around with me while I sat on it. So I rode 'Trigo' the 1929 Derby winner. Instead of paying us they would have us round to tea on a Sunday, but we never sat with the family. We would have a table of our own set aside. We knew our place.

We also helped the gamekeeper. Very often, at night, we would go out with him to catch rabbits. We put nets over the holes of burrows and then sent the ferret down. Out came the rabbits. It was nothing to catch 50-60 a night and then off to Thame to sell them at 1 shilling each'.

B.B. Romford

'Opposite our house was a slaughter house where Jim and I used to help by pulling on a rope around a beam. The bull would be on the other end, the slaughter man would then shoot the animal with a spring loaded gun, then it would be cut up. We had the job of cleaning out the stomachs out with a hosepipe. When the pigs came we would, when they were killed, pour boiling water over them and scrape the hairs off with a metal blade'.

J.B. Warrington

Golf was obviously another source of income...one method particularly dubious!!

'There was a golf course close by to where we lived and it was easily accessible via a side street. We used to lurk on the outer bounds of the golf course waiting for golf balls to be hit in our direction. Being the smallest I was poised like a rabbit out of it's trap, or a greyhound out of it's trap, ready to run across and snaffle the ball....and one of the other brothers would go round to the front of the golf house and sell the ball for

something in the region of one shilling and sixpence and that would probably take us into the cinema'.

V.M. Liverpool

Dorset Daily Echo, 6th October 1939

'To get pocket money, I worked at Woking Golf Course as a caddie and also as a kitchen boy, peeling potatoes, washing windows and running errands'.

B.M. Crawley

'For our war effort, my brother and I collected waste cardboard and paper and each weekend we would take it to the collection point in the village on a cart made by our foster parent'.

P.B. Liverpool

'Everyone was required to aid the war effort. We helped collect the aluminium pots and pans to be melted down. At school we stitched material to make wash bags for the troops in hospital. I helped in binding paper back books and made pyjama cords with the aid of a cotton reel, four nails and a crochet hook. After school and homework was done, I would help with the haymaking'.

J.R. Dartford

'Although out in the countryside was a boy's dream world for paddling, tree climbing and general fun and games, we also helped out in our Foster parents homes. They had some hens, a goat, some pigs all requiring feeding and looking after. Chaff was produced from a large rotating blade cutting through a bale of hay. Nowadays a Safety Officer would swoon if he saw it in use. Pig swill was partly made up from kitchen waste, reject vegetables etc. stored in a large barrel. Once or twice a week this mixture was transferred to an old kitchen boiler and sterilised before being mixed with commercial meal and other piggy nutrients. Not the most appetising aroma, but the pigs couldn't get enough of it!'*

R.B.

Notice to Evacuated People

THE BRIDPORT MANUFACTURERS' ASSOCIATION feel that it would be the desire of all those capable of working to be given the opportunity to render service of National Importance, rather than do nothing, at this time of emergency. Work of National Importance is available for able-bodied workers willing to learn.

Will the general public please make this fact as widely known as possible?

Wm. Edwards & Son (Bridport) Ltd.
Wm. Gale & Sons.
Joseph Gundry & Co., Ltd.
Hounsells' (Bridport) Ltd.

Wm. James & Co.
Pymore Mill Co. Ltd.
Rendall & Coombs Ltd.
Thos. Tucker & Co.

Dorset Daily Echo, 8th September 1939

homesickness

'I cried a lot in those early days, for my Mum and for my brothers and sisters and always there was Dolly (*) to mop up the tears, quite literally, for her soft body made a pillow into which I buried my head. I really did not understand anything about the war, only that my Mother had left me with these strange people'.

P.R. Maidstone

(*) Dolly was a doll.

'Christmas holidays. How happy I was to be going home, knowing that I was wanted. Time went so quickly, then it was back to Leigh and the same routine. All I was waiting for was the Easter break, then home again to London, but before I knew it I was back again. I was so home sick. I used to think 'what if there is an air-raid and my parents are killed. I won't stay here!' I wrote and told my parents how I felt and could I please come home. I always received a letter from my father with a post order on the Wednesday, but none came and I just cried and thought I would be there until the war finished. But, on the Saturday, I did receive a letter with a ten shilling note enclosed for my fare home, and a message to telling me to write to tell them what train I was getting. I couldn't wait. I immediately put all my clothes in the haversack, told my host that I was going home, went to the head teacher and then from her to the station to wait for the train to take me home to a place that I knew I would be wanted and loved'.

J.J. Bedford

'I could often be seen swinging on the garden gate in floods of tears'.

P.B. Liverpool

'My sister Irene and I were taken to Polgooth Village Hall. My mother had stipulated that my sister and I were to stay together. Because of this we were the last ones left in the hall. A lady then took us in her car to where we were to be billeted. Our foster mother was only 21 and had

115

taken us in to get the billeting money. Her husband had been called up and she had a baby of about 12 months. We had to eat the food put in front of us and this proved a problem. As we were Jewish we knew we should not eat pork, and in fact I could not eat it..........I was very homesick'.

S.B. Kent

'After about a week, my mother returned to London by coach, and for the very first time I was living away from my mother and father. Except for our usual weeks camping holiday I don't think that I had ever slept in other than my own bed. But I do not recall ever feeling really homesick. The only pain which was quite short lived was generated by a pile of weeds, would you believe!? My mother in the week she stayed had done a bit of weeding in the garden and had piled up the pickings alongside the path at the bottom of the garden. At that time they were building the houses behind Marie Road and the site was a regular playground. We accessed it over the back fence. Every time I went past that pile of weeds I saw a certain remembrance in them which generated a momentary sadness. Funny how you remember these things'.

A.K. Nottingham

'Somebody had left the catch off the door and I put my coat on the hook and as I did the door went ajar and I fell all the way down stairs on top of the coal. She must have kept all the coal there, it was pitch black. Well, of course I was crying and screaming because I had hurt my leg. I cannot remember who got me up from there but I do know they got me a chair to sit on. Then of course I was crying for me Mum, I was getting home sick. So I said to her (host) 'I want to go home!'.

She said, 'You can't go home'.

I said, 'I want me Mum' and I was crying on and on.

She said, 'I'll go round to the school and I'll ask the Head can you go home'.

So, when she went I got one of these girls to get up in the bedroom, get my haversack, my gas-mask and my tin cup, all my little belongings. They came down stairs with it and I got out of the house.

My leg still pained but I managed and I found where the bus station was in Chester....I got on the bus, haversack, gas mask and everything. I hid my face from the window of the bus in case they saw where I was and the Headmaster would come and get me and I was frightened in case a Policeman or ARP Warden would get me. Anyhow, as luck would have it, the bus went out and I thought I was safe so I started to looking through the window then to find my bearings, did I come that way or what? Anyhow, eventually the bus went to Birkenhead and I thought I know where I am now, so I got off the bus at the station. I went down the gangway, the boat was in, so I got on and it sailed. It was sailing for Liverpool and I was hiding on the boat because I was afraid in case they notified the Police and they would find me and take me back......

When the boat arrived at the Liverpool Pier Head, I walked up all the side streets. I was like a fugitive.... I walked for about 2 miles because I didn't have any money left to get on a bus. As I approached London Road I went up the other side of the street to our house. I saw my Mum on the step and I was so happy and then I paused and thought 'what will she do, will she take me back?' I was petrified but as I got closer to my Mum she said 'I was just saying to myself, I'm sure that's our Jean over there'....

Nobody came after me, nobody ever enquired about me. I was the lost Jean of Liverpool.'

J.M. Liverpool

other interest & humorous

'Farmer Jennings was in his seventies, as was his wife. There was also a housekeeper. I was puzzled by this; one lady gave me my food and the other lady darned the holes in my socks, at home Mum did both. Farmer Jennings was rather deaf and to talk to him one spoke into a metal funnel which was on a flexible metal tube which he held to his ear. After I had been there a few days his great delight was to put this appliance to my ear speak softly and then suddenly shout. How he laughed to see me give a startled jump'.

J.R. Dartford

'...One racket I was really good at was at weekends when the Mums of evacuees, not from our school, came to visit. There was yours truly, with my best uniform, putting on my best voice: "Good afternoon madam, may I carry your case? Perhaps I can direct you to where you wish to go". I only used to take them to the taxi rank, as I didn't know where anything was in Bedford anyway. That little bit of chivalry was usually good for a shilling.

I kept that up for about four weeks until somebody in authority got wind of it and a warning was given. They never found out who it was, thank goodness...

Another good little number was to go and join in the hymn singing at the Salvation Army prayer meetings, always good for tea and cake afterwards'.

D.D. Dagenham

'One thing that sticks in my mind about the war was the lack of bananas. This fruit was not available, so if a child had a father in the Navy who brought fruit home with him, they were the lucky ones. In the playground every child would stand around and watch while they peeled it and ate it. We all wanted to know what it tasted like. The skin was passed around so that we could all smell it'.

M.H. Bristol

(All imports of bananas stopped in December 1940. Some people created 'fake' bananas by cooking parsnips and mashing them in banana essence.)

Norma Campin at Downhead in 1943 and 1992

'I should not have been at Downhead at all but at Weston Super Mare, or possibly Bridgewater. Apparently, while I had been asleep on the journey all the children from St. John's School had been told to get off and I had missed it'.

N.C. Welling

'At Christmas, the school used to get a present for each girl and boy from children abroad. I remember one year getting perfume in the shape of a piano from a girl in Canada. She also sent her name and address and I wrote to her until about 1945'.

E.W. Birkenhead

'We were met at the village hall by the Rector and helpers. They were somewhat taken aback by the arrival of teenage boys. They were expecting a party of pregnant women with young children!'

E.B. Witham

Administrative mistakes like this were common and created many problems for billeting officers in the reception areas.

'*I had been in Wales for about 6 months when, believe it or not, at the age of 7, I was given call-up papers to go to war. It took Ida and Griff (hosts) a lot of paperwork to convince the Authorities that I was a seven year old evacuee. Needless to say I was convinced that I would have to go to war and Griff and Ida pulled my leg and said I would have to go, until they saw how upset it was making me*'.

H.N. Liverpool

'*Except for the somewhat core arrangements for schooling, which quickly developed into the commonplace, the only really warlike activity we took part in was air raid practice. These were initially rather desultory but got somewhat more serious as events unfurled. From both Colliton Street and the YMCA we went to different sets of open trenches.*

A letter records,

'*We have visited the trenches twice this week. The YMCA and the school trenches are camouflaged. The YMCA ones have grass and weeds growing over them and the school ones have camouflaged nets over the top*'.

The YMCA trenches were in some inner town private space, whilst the school ones were in the grounds of the County Hall. Later we used the basement of County Hall, then undergoing construction. The bottom of the trenches had lattice duck boards and I think we laid in them resting between the legs of the person in front. We never practised on rainy days!'

A.K. Nottingham

'Like many young boys of that period I took a keen interest in aircraft and could identify most allied and enemy planes. Occasionally an Avro Anson twin-engined aircraft would fly over the area, being easily recognised by their rasping Armstrong Siddeley 'Cheetah' engines. One evening a Miles Master training aircraft lost height and made an emergency landing. The Colonel (host) brought the luckless pilot to the house where he spent the night. Next morning when I heard of the incident, I hopefully left my drawing book on the hall chest with the message 'Signature of R.A.F. trainer pilot. He signed his name and drew a sketch showing foliage caught on the tail wheel of the plane. Regretfully, I never met him before I left for school that morning, but I was thrilled to have such a near encounter with a real air pilot'.

D.B. Liverpool

'Llay Picture House was our Saturday treat. We attended the matinee. But, if you ever forgot your gas-mask you were not allowed in and it was a long walk home!'

P.B. Liverpool

'My memory of the journey is a bit hazy but I do remember that there were several stops on the way, all of them I suspect due to pressure of traffic on the railways at that time. The Dunkirk evacuation was in progress and we were held up to let the troop trains through.

I can remember one stop we had due to signals that coincided with a station platform somewhere in England. A kindly porter was handing out cups of water in thick white china cups that were the style of the day. When the train started to pull out of the station I have a lasting memory of the porter haring down the platform trying to recover the cups. It was hilarious to watch some of them as he was trying to catch them and missed...'

D.P. (no address)

'Water had to be carried every night in earthenware pitchers from the village pump (Hewas Water. Cornwall). All the men would gather there at about 7 .00pm to have a chat and eventually carry the water home. No one had piped water. There were no sewers and we used a toilet at the end

of the garden which had a bucket in it. This had to be emptied and the contents were buried at the end of the garden. This toilet was always very clean. Off course, there was no light in it and it was a bit scary in the dark winter afternoons and evenings'.

S.B. Kent

'In 1940, Mrs T. said that my sister Joan could come to live with us where I would be responsible for her. Joan was 6 years old then and had a been handicapped through Polio from the age of two, she wore a Calliper and a built up shoe.

Being responsible for Joan could be frustrating at times. When there was a full moon she would sing hymns at the top of her voice and certainly took no notice of me asking her to be quiet. That meant I was in trouble for letting her wake everyone up.

We thought that perhaps she couldn't help this behaviour, but she has told me in recent years that she did it on purpose to get me into trouble!'

M.G. Crowborough

'During the war, Bootle, where I lived with my parents and twin brother, was subject to very heavy bombing and as my father was in the forces and our house had been hit, my mother, twin brother and I were evacuated to the Isle of Man.

Although I was very young, I still have quite vivid memories of men being paraded behind barbed wire. I knew they were not soldiers because none of them wore military uniform and the word 'internee' was not in my vocabulary'.

S.H. Ormskirk

'I had been a scout in Rochester and (as an evacuee) joined the 1st Hythe Sea Scouts. Our Headquarters was right on the beach, next to the Coastguards' lookout building and we spent some of our weekend time acting as lookouts and messengers. We saw a number of British and German aircraft shot down and their crews ditch into the sea just off the coast.

Then in 1940 came the BEF evacuation from Dunkirk. Our Scout Troop's 40ft motor cruiser had been laid up at the outbreak of war because of petrol rationing but had been scrupulously maintained under the instruction of our Skipper, a retired Royal Navy Officer. The call came for small boats to assist in the evacuation and Skip immediately volunteered our craft. It was extremely seaworthy and in immaculate condition. It was quickly fuelled and provisioned and every boy wanted to go on this great adventure. Of course, for most of us it was out of the question and Skip and another leader took our cruiser to join the hundreds of little ships heading for Dunkirk. Their adventures were used as background material for Percy Westerman's book 'Sea Scouts Alert'.

J.H. Reading

'Some of the evacuees were in hospital for a while, they found some explosives and threw them in a fire and burnt their faces, they walked around with masks for sometime. We used to go to the Co-op and buy blocks of blood for one penny. They were called penny ducks and we ate them. The blood was dried in a tray and cut into squares about one and a half inches square'.

J.B. Warrington

'Dorchester....was definitely country. I have never subsequently really got across to anyone else the quite subtle impact that seeing cowpats had on me. In terms that I wouldn't have used at the time, they seemed to me to be the icons of rural life'.

A.K. Nottingham

'I can remember the L.D.V. (*) drilling with their broomsticks wearing civilian clothes, with their khaki armbands on in the Recreation area. During one exercise they set up an ambush in a derelict building in the west end of Abercarn, known to us as the Chapel of Ease. This ambush was supposed to be secret, but a group of us kids got to hear of it and sat on the wall opposite, laughing, joking and generally taking the mickey out of them. They in turn, in no uncertain manner, told us what we should be doing with ourselves. Although something of a joke at the time, each of these men were prepared to lay down their lives for their country'.

D.P.

(*) Local Defence Volunteers, later the Home Guard.

'Dorchester also introduced me to a sense of the past. Even at the age of nine, one had some perception of 1066 and all that, and there had been lots of Kings and Queens in the past. But they could all be a myth as far as my perhaps disinterested experience could prove. But in Dorchester there were Roman ruins ex-stock, and just outside it was the iron-age fort of Maiden Castle.....I was no eager buff of these things and to this day my interest is short of intense, but in a time where extensive travelling was not the norm, these awarenesses gave light to new horizons. For all that I do recall being somewhat chastened when we were told that we were going to see a Roman villa, to find nothing above the ground, higher than about 18"
. My long term interest in ruins took a near fatal blow!'.

A.K. Nottingham

'After school, I remember we'd look longingly at chocolate bars in a village shop window. We finally snitched one but all we got for our trouble was a big let down. After eagerly unwrapping our ill-gotten gain, we found it was only a wooden dummy, for display purposes only'.

M.K. Ontario

The following account from a teacher describes the problems he faced when wishing to move the school into larger accommodation. He and his school had been evacuated to a small village in Berkshire where, the existing village school buildings, although cramped, had been adequate. When extra families arrived it was necessary to move to bigger premises and he sought the permission of the local Rector to move into the semi-derelict, wooden, church hall at the opposite end of the village to the school. It was not until the spring of 1940 that the evacuees were able to move and one afternoon the older boys carried the desks along the main street followed by the juniors carrying books and chairs. Over the weekend the pupils cut down the hedges, tidied the paths, put up temporary notice boards and hung pictures and maps on the wall to make them a little more presentable. On the Monday the teacher sat the class according to size....smallest at the front, largest at the back. The rest is worth describing in his own words:-

"I gave the order to stand, with the idea of marking the occasion of the move with a little ceremony.

'Well school,' I began, ' here we are in our new home...'

Suddenly the floor began gently to subside and rows of children sank before my eyes like little ships going down. A few books slid off desks and one or two children sat down, standing up quickly again as though they had done something wrong; the smaller ones clung to their desks and everyone stood a little lopsidedly, but they were calm and left it to the stupidest senior to state the obvious.

'Please sir,' he said, ' the floor's guv away.'

So we all went home."

GASMASKS FOR ANIMALS
EVEN AN ELEPHANT CAN BE FITED

A firm of manufacturers is now prepared to make gasmasks for any animal - even an elephant. The manager told a reporter that nearly all animals could be given the same degree of immunity from gas attacks as a human being.

"The extraordinary thing about it" he said, "is that, most animals show less objection to wearing masks than do men and women. It does not seem to worry them. When I first began to try my masks on horses I put some hay in the bottom of them so that they might think that it was a nosebag, but they never ate the hay and took it all so placidly that I soon discontinued the practice."

Masks for dogs and cats are made in eight sizes and are fitted with slide fasteners and adjustable neck straps. It is claimed they can be put on in 30 seconds. No matter how vigorously the dog shakes his head, he cannot dislodge the mask.

OUTLET VALVES FITTED

The masks are easier to breath in than the human type because they are fitted with outlet as well as inlet valves. For a shire horse the inlet valve is as big as a large paint can and weighs two pounds.

Oiled fabric is used for the sides instead of rubber material because it is stronger. Even a cat's sharp claws could not puncture it easily.

The manager began experimenting with the animal gasmasks six years ago and has sent a great number to Spain, Poland, Czechoslovakia, Sweden, Belgium and Holland.

Dorset Daily Echo, 7th March 1940

Homes Wanted For Evacuated Pets

Greatest problem of many evacuees has been what to do with their pets. Dogs and cats homes in London could not cope with the rush and many people had no time to make arrangements for themselves.

To their rescue has come the Animal Defence Society which has, in a very short time, organised a smoothly working animal evacuation scheme. Already hundreds of cats and dogs have been sent out of London to carefully chosen homes in the country and more are leaving every day.

Duchess of Hamilton, who is president of the society, stated she was overwhelmed with pets wanting temporary homes in the country.

"I have sent hundreds to my house in Dorset (Ferne. Shaftsbury) and many more to homes in all parts of the country, but I am still in urgent need of more animal lovers who will be prepared to look after cats and dogs. If people can afford it they pay for the keep, but in many cases those we are helping are too poor, so we urgently need people who can afford to look after an animal without payment."

"If any of your readers would like an animal for the time being, I can promise them plenty to choose from, and they will know they are making some poor person very happy and really doing something to help their country."

Anyone who would like to help the Duchess should write to her at 25, St Edmunds Terrace. N.W.8 marking the envelope 'Homes' and she will give them further details.

Swanage Times, 2nd November 1939

127

air raid

'I had been evacuated in May 1940 to Hindhead in Surrey, but in September of that year my mother decided we would go to Wiltshire for a holiday. It was arranged that I would come home on the Friday and on the Saturday we would travel to Wiltshire. That was one holiday that never did come off. My home was in North Woolwich with the Royal Docks just across the road almost and the Woolwich Arsenal over the water, so it wasn't likely to be overlooked for long by the Luftwaffe! Unfortunately for me they chose that very week end that I was home.

I hadn't been in the house very long before the sirens went and I experience my first air raid. We went out to the shelter which was a brick built affair of one room, the Authorities having decided that if it was hit there wouldn't be too many bricks to fall on us and if the house was hit the shelter would protect us. Anyway, as far as I was concerned all hell broke loose as the ships in the Docks opened fire and bombs fell. My mother's view was that it hadn't been too bad, it was soon over. But it turned out to be an introduction to what was to follow the next day, Saturday.

They came around midday, following the River Thames. No sirens announced the bombers. A black cloud of bombers surrounded by silver fighters just somehow quietly and unexpectedly appeared in the sky above us. At first when I saw them I thought they were ours because the sirens hadn't gone. I was only eleven years old but already had great faith in the RAF.

Through that afternoon they bombed us. The ships guns fired. A gun that I was told was called a 'Mobile Gun' seemed to rush up and down the street firing madly. A bomb was dropped two doors away that wiped out all the top half of our street.

My mother and I can remember this so clearly, decided to go and see if she could help. I clung to her crying that she couldn't leave her only child. She removed my hands and said I would be safe with my grandparents. The people might need help and she would be back. All was as she said. My grandmother first putting a blanket over my head and quoting from the Bible that fire would destroy the world.

129

It didn't exactly help!!

When the 'all clear' went at about 6.30pm and we came out of the shelter, I thought she was right. The whole of North Woolwich seemed to be on fire and there was no gas, electricity or water pressure to fight the fires. They had set fire to our beautiful church, St. John the Evangelist, and we stood and watched. The Rev. Garcia was out on ARP duties.

It was decided to leave North Woolwich. We knew the bombers would come back. We were going to my Aunt who lived in Plumstead and it was decided that my grandfather would go on ahead and we would follow. To get across the river you went by ferry or walked through the tunnel that runs under the River Thames. Obviously at that time no ferries were in use, so we set out for the tunnel. My mother was the Police Matron at the local Police Station and so had to report to them to say where we were going. That delay kept us in the tunnel all night!

As we went down the steps the sirens went and the gates were closed. We walked through to the South Woolwich side and a young policeman who should have gone off duty at 10pm found he had company for the night! He found a ladder for the women and children to sit on, rigged up a toilet, using a bucket and made tea with about a teaspoon of tea leaves. My mother always said that he deserved a medal.

Right through the night the bombs fell, some seemed very close but the policeman assured us that they were miles away.

At 6am the 'all clear' went and the gates were opened and in rushed the men who had come off the 10pm shift at the Arsenal, but of course could not get across the river to their families and homes. They wanted to know what was happening in North Woolwich, but we didn't know either. To them and to me looking down from the hill, it seemed that no one could survive. The whole area seemed to be on fire.

People did survive though. I went back to Hindhead. My grandparents evacuated to relatives in Wiltshire and my mother went back to our house and her job at the Police Station. There she not only carried out her duties as Police Matron but also kept the canteen open all night for the bomb disposal groups and others, when nobody else could be found to do it.

E.H. Harpenden

'I was born in Stepney and was 5 when the war started. My mother, in her wisdom, decided that if we were going to die then we should all die together, that meant aunts and cousins as well. We stayed in London during the Blitz, going each afternoon to the big warehouse at the docks, from the outside sunlight to the dark cave which was the warehouse, with a minute light at the other end which led out to the docks.

All through the night the wardens were bringing dead and wounded in and shouting 'women and children turn your heads'. In the morning we walked home through waist high piles of broken glass back to Sidney Street'.

J.F. Surrey

'In June 1944 I was living with my parents, my 17 year old sister and my 11 year old brother at 65 Craven Gardens, Wimbledon, South West 19, in a small Edwardian semi-detached house which my parents had rented for £1 17s 6d a week from a private landlord. My father worked as a wages secretary to Keir, the concrete building magnate. Keir's moved their office operation from the East End of London to a large house on Wimbledon Hill in 1940 to avoid the bombing. My father moved the family over from Lewisham to keep his job going. When the doodle-bugs started falling in mid-June 1944 we had a Morrison table shelter in the downstairs rooms in our secluded road. It was the practice at that particular time for Mums to keep their front doors open when they were home during the day and if the kids were playing in the road....

At 6 years old I was the youngest child in our gang and as soon as the air raid siren sounded the alert we would run like hell for the nearest open door and under the table shelter.....One particular bright cloudy day in mid-morning, my mother was at home and a few of us children were playing English and Germans in our front gardens and side passages. When the sirens went off we ran to the house. Our front door faced directly South so the flying bombs would always come over Tooting and Streatham direction and we would usually hear the sirens going over their districts before ours. Our siren was on the roof of the Wimbledon Police Station at the top of Queen's Road. It is difficult to describe now the stereophonic or surround sound when all the districts' four or five sirens and the others further away were sounding off at the same time.

We heard this particular doodle-bug coming quickly from the usual direction. We had only heard V1s before but had not seen one. We knew Mum was up the road so being curious we stopped in our doorway and waited for it to pass overhead. The noise was terrific and it was very low as it sped over the roof tops opposite from left to right. The echo of it came at us from all directions......Just as the doodle-bug had gone over, my mother came down the pavement showing her legs up to her thighs. She was a fairly modest person...and up to that time I had never seen her legs, now she pulled up her skirt as mothers do during the Mums' races during the school sports days. Now as she ran through our front gate she shouted and pushed us into the front hall passage. The engine of the Doodle bug cut out just as we took cover. Lots of descriptions of the cut out and the bang, lots of descriptions have been given about those few seconds of silence between the cut out and the bang of a V1. I experienced this heart stopping moment myself 3-4 times. My recollection is that when the nearby revolting noise of the pulse jet engine was so loud that when it cut out over the buildings there was a long round-the-houses echo for a second or two.

As we crouched or lay in the Morrison shelter I remember thinking, 'It's going to be all right, it's not for us' had we got it I would never have had cause to regret being wrong. When we survived I could rejoice at being right. The thought of being permanently injured didn't even occur to me. On this occasion there were 3 of us children, my mother and our Alsatian dog, under the Morrison shelter when the bomb went off with a terrific resounding bang, way over the back of the house.....Some of our open windows cracked and items fell off the shelves and the mantelpieces. After settling down her own group, except the dog, for whom bangs made no impression, my mother went to comfort a neighbour with brandy from medicine bottle kept for such purposes.

Later after a bad night of doodle bugs in late June 1944 we heard that our school in Ephra (sic) Road had been bomb damaged. We went down with Mum to Faraday Road to view the damage....The flying bomb had brought down 10 houses in the road and rescue lorries were still in attendance....we were overjoyed..no more school.

It was ten years later that I was told by a carpenter for the rescue squads at that time, that they were still looking for the dead and injured on the morning we were watching.

Soon after this incident a lady in uniform came to our front door and told my mother that my brother Graham and I were to be evacuated with the rest of the children in our district and that we would have to present ourselves at Wimbledon Station....'

V.S. London

'During the summer of 1944 I well remember listening to a news broadcast in the doorway of a shop called Stones, they were a branch of a multi-retail wireless shop, announcing that our troops had landed on the continent early that morning. The pal I was with and I then cycled back to school which was Southall County School. It was not long after that we were told, on the wireless and by the newspapers, of the advent of the Doodlebugs, which we knew by sight and sound anyway.

Our lessons were continually being interrupted by the sirens and we would all troop to the air-raid shelters.

I was doing a paper round before school and used to watch them fly over. Provided the motors did not cut out before they reached your position you knew you were OK.

One night a Doodlebug landed on Southall Park within a hundred yards of the school and blew in the Chemistry, Physics and Biology Labs. Much to the annoyance of we boys, it had fallen short and not landed on the school so we would not have had to attend classes. Such is the thinking of teenage boys. Because of this, my parents decided that my sister and I should be evacuated. She went to Yorkshire and I to Nottinghamshire........

The correspondent returned to London and went through this experience just after his return....

'A few days later, it was still the school summer holiday, I spent the morning laying on a chaise-longue which was under a large window and as Doodlebugs went over I would get under the table if it sounded as if the motor would cut out. I had finished the book I was reading and decided to cycle to the library, which was less than a mile away. I had just got there when a Doodlebug approached and its motor cut out. I laid down, as everyone was told to do, in the entrance to the library and as it exploded

and small flakes of plaster fell on me, I thought to myself ' That was close!' There were two books that I wanted to read, probably Biggles, however I could only take one out so I stayed and read one. I then left and cycled home with the other. As I neared the road where I lived I realised that, in modern parlance, there had been an incident. The Doodlebug had landed fifty yards or so away from our house which was badly damaged. My mother and father had been summoned from work, everyone was worried as to my whereabouts. The chaise-longue was speared by a large shaped piece of glass. It was fortunate that I had finished my book at the right time'.

C.H. Tylers Green

'January 2nd 1941 is a date etched in my memory because, after avoiding heavy air raids for many months, this was the evening Hitler's bombs caught up with me. My aunt, who was an infant teacher, had also been evacuated with her school, Barnsole Road School, Gillingham, to Maesycwmmer and latterly to Bedwas. She set off to visit my parents and myself in Barry but unfortunately picked up the wrong suitcase from the bus in which she was travelling. It belonged to someone in Caerphilly. My mother, Aunt and myself decided to return the suitcase to the owner. We set out from Barry to Cardiff after lunch on that January day thence to Caerphilly. By this time it was dusk and it was snowing. We arrived at the address, exchanged the suitcases, but on our return by bus over Caerphilly mountain to Cardiff were appalled to discover we were being taken into the city in the middle of a heavy air-raid. There was a red glow over Cardiff that could be seen for miles.

We headed for the air-raid shelter as soon as the bus stopped at the City Hall; stayed for a few hours, then made our way to Cardiff Castle where there were more shelters within the castle walls (they were of course extremely thick) stepping over frozen hosepipes that were drawing water from the canal and eventually, when the 'All-Clear' sounded reached a bus stop for Barry. We arrived home in a fleet of buses that had been sent out to pick up people stranded by the air-raid, to be received by my frantic father at two o'clock in the morning'.

M.H-J. Glamorgan

letters back home

The following are extracts from letters which evacuees sent home during their time away. Some have only recently been found.

'3 January 1940,

Dear Mum and Dad,

Thanks for parcel very much, in your letter you said Heinz has enclosed some sweets (*) ....The pen is quite a good one which you sent as I hope you can see. The puzzles you send us were jolly good and the next time you see Mr Bishop please would you thank him very much (§).

On Monday we went and saw some silent films and on Tuesday we saw a talkie film and in the afternoon we had our tea party. We had some games and I won 4d and a 2d bar of chocolate. We had a big tea also 3 cakes, 2 buns, 4 rolls and a cup of lemonade...I don't know but would you send me my 5/- Frog Aeroplane. I'll pay for the stamps. Brian has a frog plane. It is a model of a Vickers Wellesly. It has had several crashes going into houses and fences.

Cheerio

Alec.'

(*) Heinz was the correspondent's lodger at his home. He was a German Jew who worked for Mullards in Mitcham. He was subsequently detained under Regulation 18B and the family lost contact with him.

(§) Mr Bishop owned the London removal company whose vans are still to be seen nation-wide under the slogan 'Bishop's Move'.

27 March 1940

Dear Mum and Dad,

Thankyou for your letter and sixpence. Uncle went back this afternoon after his Easter leave. He caught the 2 o'clock train.

On Tuesday we played two games of football. We won one 2-nil and drew the other 0-0. We also had a game this afternoon but lost 4-1. What a score!

Last Saturday my friend's Dad, who had come to see him, took me to Weymouth and Portland. We saw a lot of merchant ships and a few destroyers and on Monday he took me to Lulworth as I suppose you know by the card I sent you. On top of one of the cliffs there is a little Coast Guard station, and far out at sea we saw a British submarine, signal by a Morse searchlight to the Coast Guards. The last we saw of it disappeared heading for Portland.

If the weather is fine tomorrow we are going to Weymouth with the school, but we have to pay our own fees.

The pen I am writing with is a tanner Woolies, Woolworths, fountain pen. It is not a bad one as it has written this whole letter with one dip in the ink.

Cheerio

Alec.'

'MAY DAY. MARCHANTS HILL SCHOOL CAMP. HINDHEAD. 20 May 1942

My Darling Mum.

Thankyou for the parcel, especially the sweets and the milk chocolate. I am writing the poem 'IF' by Rudyard Kipling for you as you said you would like it.

Can I come home on June 6th for a week, if so please send me letters enclosing money.

We are going OK for 'May Day'. We have our four allies. Pat Clare is Canada, Pat Jennings is China, Gwen Read is America and I am Russia.

The four seasons are Winter, Shiela Foulds. Spring, Iris Moody. Summer, Jean Margeram and Autumn, Doris Grundy.

I am going to enclose my speech later.

Eileen.

The following letter is unusual in that it was written by an 18 year old schoolgirl to the Minister of Education in September 1942. She was motivated to write it in response to a great deal of adverse criticism of the evacuation scheme in the press at that time. The letter was found in 1974 by the correspondent's war-time host when she was moving house.

'2 September 1942

Dear Sir,

Three years ago today found my mother, small sister and myself, then aged 15, being evacuated by the Government from a London suburb to this small East Anglian village. On first setting out I was a very rebellious character, declaring that I was certain I should return home within a few days. Today finds me still here in my original billet!

When I arrived I was determined to continue my education, but there seemed to be no school of the same kind as that which I had left at home. Thus, after some weeks spent assisting with some infant evacuees in the village Hut, I was admitted to the Pupil Teacher's Centre, four miles away.

My first year was not without difficulties, but nevertheless a happy one. Evacuees gradually returned home, until I alone remained. At the end of the summer term I gained my School Certificate and the time had come, as I feared, when my school days were to end. By this time however, I had grown to love the country and the prospect of having to go to business, in a London office for example, was not a pleasant one.

So, after much consideration, it was agreed that I should be allowed to take up a specially reduced apprenticeship as a Pupil Teacher. Hence I embarked on a further two years of school life. That apprenticeship has now ended and thanks to the help of the Essex Education Committee and the fact that I have been awarded one of the very few scholarships available, it is now possible for me to enter a Training College at the end of this month.

Ever since I have been evacuated, peculiar though it may seem, I have been a member of the Young Farmers' Club, of which I am now secretary of this particular branch. In June this year, I was successful in a County Stock Judging competition. I have also taken part in Youth Service activities.

People may argue that country life is dull, but I shall always disagree. I have never had an idle moment since I arrived. As for the question 'Is evacuation a success?' I consider that it can be. Had it not been for the War and evacuation, I should never have had the opportunity to follow the teaching profession. I have learnt of the country ways and customs and indulged in interesting things. Harvest time has found me doing various jobs on a nearby farm, from stooking corn to tractor driving. I have met interesting and important people through the Young Farmers' Club, among which has been the Minister of Agriculture himself. Above all I have made many firm friends.

I wish to thank the Ministry for having taken such an excellent measure as is evacuation. Thousands say 'a failure', but if both evacuees and receivers will only cooperate, I am confident that it can be a real success. I perhaps was unusually fortunate in being received into a home as one of the family and where I have been treated with great kindness, for which I am deeply grateful. Nevertheless, I see no reason why others should not find evacuation as successful and enjoyable as it has been for me.

It has changed my whole outlook on life and I cannot but feel that it is for the good. I can only leave my reader to decide whether or not this is an advertisement for successful evacuation.

Yours sincerely,

J.I.'

J.G. Suffolk

(This correspondent, like many other evacuees, returned to live in the village she was originally evacuated to. However, she never did receive a reply, or any acknowledgement from the Ministry!)

^Apersonal story through letters

I am indebted to Keith Wilson for allowing me to use extracts from the letters he and his teachers/guardians wrote to his parents during the war. Keith was evacuated to Bovey Tracey in South Devon. Although things get off to a good start Keith does, like many others, feel homesick after a few weeks in his billet.

EVACUATION to a big country house has meant good living for these London boys. Their hostess (centre) and her servants look after them, and for meals they sit on tapestry chairs and eat as much as they want off an oilcloth-covered mahogany dining-table under the peaceful gaze of the figures in a valuable oil painting.

Sunday Express, 10th September 1939 - Keith is second from right

'6.9.39

Dear Mum,

The house I am staying at has a big quarry at the back with woods on the top, with plenty of rocks to hide in. One of my school pals lives at the bottom of our lane. Will you please send me a postal order for 1/6 as I am running out of money'.

26th.

Dear Mum,

I have had a bit of earache in the last few days, a perforated eardrum. I have to got to hospital everyday'.

4th October 1939

Dear Mr Wilson,

I have seen Keith and have had a quiet talk with him and am very pleased to be able to say that he is now quite recovered from his ear trouble, is quite fit, and says that he is quite happy and content. I think that his discontent was born partly of the discomfort from his ear trouble and in fact homesickness. I did not let him know that you had written to me, but he would like to see you both and I do not think that it would cause him to be unhappy when you went back. Keith is quite old enough and is sensible enough to understand that Devon is, at present, a much nicer place to be in than Acton. I asked him whether you would be visiting him or not and said that he did not know. Further, I asked him whether he would ask to be taken back if you came down and he said that he did not want to go back as he was very happy here.

Keith forms one of the party of ten boys and three masters at Whitstone House, a big house standing in its own grounds on a hillside having a most lovely view over to Haytor and the Moors. The boys are extremely well fed, have very good beds in large rooms and have plenty of safe but exercising play room in the grounds. Mr Papineau, who is in charge, is running the place on Boarding school lines and has grace before meals, evening prayers, cleanliness inspections and a proper rota for hot baths. Mrs Farquharson, the owner of Whitstone, is extremely nice and kind to the boys and it is doing them all a tremendous lot of good in every way. Keith could not be better placed as regards billeting.

I hope to be able to get to town for the week-end on October 14th and if I can will call on you then.

Yours truly.

R.Ebbetts.'

Dear Mum,

I do not like it here very much. I feel homesick. I want to come home. Hope everyone is well and happy.

Love to all

Keith.

PS I mean it.

But obviously his attention was soon taken up playing with his Meccano sets...

'Dear Mum,

Will you please buy me No.1a Meccano outfit which will cost about 2/6. For 1/10 please buy me 2 Armstrong Whitworth bomber Dinky toys. ....

With my Meccano I made a breakdown car and one boy has got a Meccano aeroplane constructor outfit....'

'Dear Mum,

......I am getting 2 Meccano sets. 1a and 2a making mine into 3. Will you send my clockwork motor down please and all the parts you can find. There are two flanged plates...'

There was also an explanation from his headmaster as to the reason behind his homesickness. This correspondence is very rare, and historically important, as few such letters from hosts/teachers have survived.

'4 October 1939

Dear Mr and Mrs Wilson,

It is with great pleasure that I acknowledge both your letters to me. I do not however apologise for the delay. It is, I think, quite obvious that an investigation such as you asked me to undertake, namely, the finding of the reason for Keith's apparent homesickness, cannot be completed in a week or two. And to be perfectly frank with you it is not yet finally finished but the material facts and conclusions are before me and the rest is merely a matter of detail.

If I may be as brief as is possible under the circumstances (since I do not want to bore you with the technicalities) Keith's trouble is one which will naturally right itself in the course of time and with the minimum of interference or of sympathy on behalf of either you or myself. You must, and I think you do, understand that all of us are now engaged in a type of living which is absolutely foreign to the majority of our natures. Some of us are more adaptable than others. Some of us have perhaps experienced previously conditions similar to these. I for instance was in the Scouts for seven or eight years, camping two or three times a year with scores of other children of my own age.

None of the ten boys under my care here, to my knowledge, experienced that. It follows therefore that living together as they are, these boys are getting intimate glimpses of each other's lives, their private lives mark you, and in some cases it hurts. I should say, quite rightly I believe, and without being at all snobbish, that Keith is with those boys who are, if I may use the term, refined. However, it takes all sorts to make a world and there are other boys with us who are not so refined. You may say that Keith was with them at school. Certainly he was but he didn't wash, eat, sleep, pray and play with them. All of us I think are in the same boat. The boys are probably learning things about their teachers which they never knew before. Moreover, some of the characteristics newly discovered by these youngsters among themselves may be good or they may be not so good. I say 'not so good' advisedly because I can assure you there is not one bad, really bad, boy with us. They were hand-picked by me to begin with and I am very capable in my selections as a rule.

I hope I have made my point perfectly clear. Keith's trouble is only the natural outcome of being literally torn from those he loves and understands, and having to live with comparative strangers and individuals of his own age who have little inter-sentimental feeling.

I feel perfectly certain that when Keith has had the time and patience to adjust himself to this new set of circumstances he will be perfectly happy here. He is growing more reconciled and more like himself day by day.

In conclusion, may I be permitted to state that Keith is, unknown to himself, probably doing work of which you personally will feel proud. I stated at the outset of my letter that Keith was among the more refined group. This group is having a most beneficial influence on the others. Their manners, behaviour, speech and general deportment are improving day by day, and it is thanks to such boys as Keith that these necessary improvements are being made possible.

I sincerely hope and trust that you will carry on in exactly the same sensible way you are doing, writing Keith as often as possible, sending him books and games and generally treating him as you always treated him. I can assure you he will come back to you all the better for his experience and with an outlook broadened by the people with whom he is in daily contact.

Believe me to be,

Yours very sincerely,

R.J. Papineau.'

formal communications

Some schools were forced to re-evacuate because the areas they had gone to became the subject of enemy attacks. This happened to the Mitcham County Schools which had originally been evacuated to Weston-Super-Mare but then took the decision to return to London.

'Mitcham County School at Weston-Super-Mare.

7 July 1942

Dear Parent,

After the recent air raids on Weston-Super-Mare there have had to be alterations in the arrangements of this school.

Owing to the damage done to the school here, the Somerset Education Committee feel that they can no longer offer us the use of the buildings in Weston which we have so far enjoyed.

The decision for each child must be left in the parents hands.

Should you decide to leave him or her here in Weston, arrangements will be made for continued secondary education at one of the local county schools.

Should you wish for re-evacuation to another reception area, it can be arranged and suitable provision will be made in the new area for continued education.

Should you decide to have your child back in Mitcham the Boys and Girls County Schools will open for instruction at all stages of school life, including the 6th form. I think it likely that all members of the present staff here will be available for service in Mitcham next term.

The school here will close for instruction on or about 24 July. The school in Mitcham will open 15 September, there is no reason why those whose parents decide to have them back in Mitcham should return immediately term breaks up, that entitled to remain evacuated until their return is arranged......

We were grateful that there was no injury to a child of this school, and I know that parents will be glad to know that their behaviour both during and after the raid has been excellent.

London University are fully aware of the effect that the raids may have had on Examination candidates and will make all allowances possible.

I should be glad if you would write to me and give me your decision as soon as possible so that I may make the necessary plans.

In particular I hope those parents who had been thinking of sixth form work for their boy or girl will not allow these changes to affect the decision adversely.

Yours sincerely,

A.J. Doig'.

MINISTRY OF HEALTH

WHITEHALL, S.W.1

You are among the many fathers and mothers
who wisely took advantage of the Government's
scheme to send their children to the country.
I am sorry to learn that some parents are
now bringing their children back.
I am writing to ask you not to do this.
This is not easy, for family life has always
been the strength and pride of Britain.
But I feel it my duty to remind you
that to bring children back to the congested
towns is to put them in danger of death or
what is perhaps worse, maiming for life.
You will have noticed that the Enemy is
changing his tactics.
He is now concentrating heavier air raids on
one or two towns at a time, leaving others
alone for the moment.
Nobody knows which town he will attack next.

So don't be lulled into a false sense of security if your home district has been having a quieter time lately.

Remember that in April over 600 children under sixteen were killed and over 500 seriously injured in air raids.
So keep your children where they are in the reception areas.
Don't bring them back even for a little while.
This is your duty to the children themselves, to the A.R.P. Services in your home town, to those who are working so hard for them in the country, and to the nation.
Please read this message as the sincere words of a friend both to you and to the little ones.

Yours sincerely,

Ernest Brown.

AN overseas case-study

I am indebted to Patricia Johnston for allowing me to quote the following formal correspondence between her parents, living in Liverpool at the time, and the C.O.R.B. authorities.

Patricia sailed on the 'M.S. Batory'. This ship, built at Trieste in 1936, was, until war broke out, regularly making trans-Atlantic journeys from Gydnia to New York. She was first pressed into service as a troop carrier in the Atlantic, North Sea and the Mediterranean and then used to transfer £40m worth of gold bullion from England's gold reserves to Canada for safe-keeping.

On 6 August, 1940 she left Liverpool to take 480 evacuees to Australia. The journey, which should have been 13,000 miles, was actually a 20,000 mile trip as the ship crossed the equator three times in order to avoid U-boats and mine fields. There was added danger in that the ship was also carrying nearly a thousand troops which would have made it a legitimate target for enemy action.

These letters are very important as they demonstrate the after-care that C.O.R.B. offered to parents with evacuees overseas. However, some of the Government letters also demonstrate the bureaucratic procedures which parents had to comply with at this time.

The letters are in sequential order:-

Notice, in this first letter, the stress on maintaining secrecy!

Telephone:
Mayfair 8400.

Dear Sir (or Madam),

I am writing this personal letter on the instructions of
Geoffrey Shakespeare who is the Minister responsible for the ad-
ministration of the Children's Overseas Reception Scheme. Mr.
Shakespeare is sure that you will appreciate its reassuring
nature.

You may have heard over the wireless, or have read in the
Press, that the Government cannot take responsibility for sending
children overseas under the scheme without adequate naval
protection.

In the accompanying letter you are informed that your child
(children) has (have) been accepted for evacuation overseas.
This does not necessarily mean that they will be sailing at an
early date but only that they have been placed on the waiting
list from which children are selected as and when shipping
accommodation becomes available. You should, therefore, make no
special preparations until you have had further notification.
This will be either direct from the Board if your child(children)
is(are) at a non-grant aided school or from the Local Education
Authority if at a grant-aided school. When you receive that
notification you may conclude that the ship in which your child
(children) is(are) to sail will be convoyed. If at the very
last moment there were to be a sudden change in the situation
and the Admiralty informed the Board that the ship could not,
after all, be convoyed, the arrangements for the sailing would be
cancelled forthwith and you would be duly notified.

In the interest of the safety of your child(children), and
others who will accompany them, we ask you to regard this
information as confidential - that is to say, you should not
discuss the matter even with your neighbours, and you should
ask your child(children) also not to talk about it. We know
we can rely upon you in this matter.

Yours faithfully,

S.D.L. 18(R)

The accompanying letter referred to above covered four main points...

FOR RETENTION BY PARENTS

It is important that you should read the attached letter <u>very carefully.</u>

The main points are

1. That consent to the sending of the child must be given by persons having proper authority to give it.

2. That the child will be sent at the risk of the persons who make the application.

3. That the Government will do their best for the child but cannot accept responsibility for him or her.

4. That the parents or guardians will be liable to make the payments mentioned in paragraph 4 of the letter.

If when you receive the attached letter you have not got the consent of any absent parent or guardian whose consent is required, you are advised to ask the absent parent or guardian to send it <u>to you</u> by telegram or letter.

It is realised that many fathers are absent with one of the Services and in such cases special consideration will be given to them, but you can help by following closely the instructions contained in the notice appended to the form.

The "Form of Application and Acceptance of Terms" should be returned in the enclosed envelope as soon as possible. Delay may result if it is not returned within 48 hours.

It is interesting to note that the Government were not prepared to accept the responsibility for the safety of the children whilst in their care!

LIVERPOOL EDUCATION COMMITTEE.

SCHOOL MEDICAL DEPARTMENT.

MUNICIPAL ANNEXE.

DALE STREET. LIVERPOOL. 2.

W. M. FRAZER,
O.B.E., M.D.,M.SC.,D.P.H.,
Medical Officer to the
Education Authority

TELEPHONE CENTRAL 5480.

Our Ref.............................

Your Ref.............................

4 JUL 1940

Dear Sir or Madam,

      Voluntary Scheme for the Evacuation of School
                Children Overseas.

      With reference to the registration of your child
Patricia P. McGrath, under the above Scheme,
it will be necessary for the child to attend at the
School Clinic, Sugnall Street, off Myrtle Street (opposite
the Eye and Ear Infirmary) on _Monday_, the
8 JUL 1940, at _10.0am_. The child must be
accompanied by a responsible parent or guardian.

      This medical inspection is an essential part of
the scheme and no child will be considered for acceptance
by the Dominions Authorities unless such an examination
has been carried out.

                      Yours faithfully,

                          W. M. FRAZER,

                      Medical Officer to the
                      Education Authority.

CHILDREN'S OVERSEAS RECEPTION BOARD

Tel: Mayfair 8400

45, Berkeley Street,
W.1.

Ref:- 355   January, 1941

Dear Sir/Madam

    I am glad to be able to tell you that

        Patricia is

now living with

    Mrs. William Fisher,
      135, Bell Street,
          Preston,
            Victoria.

    I hope that you will now be receiving

letters regularly and that

    Patricia is

settling down happily.

        Yours faithfully,

        Elspeth Dennes

CHILDREN'S OVERSEAS RECEPTION BOAR[D]

GMG.

C.O.R.B. Reference:

PLEASE QUOTE MAX 355.

Your Reference:

45, BERKELEY STREE[T]

Telegrams:
Avoncorb, London.

Telephone:
MAYFAIR 8400

3rd February, 194[1]

Dear Sir,

I thank you for your le[tter]
addressed to Miss Maxse.

I am very glad to note [that]
you are receiving such good news [for]
your daughter.

You ask about her C.O.R[.B.]
Number, this is 355. We shall be
glad if you will always quote this
Number when writing to us.

Yours faithfully,

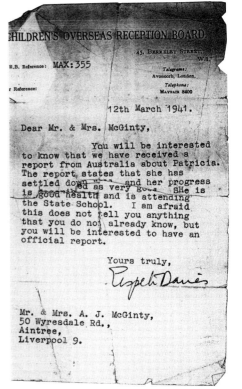

Arthur J.McGinty,Esq.,

CHILDREN'S OVERSEAS RECEPTION BOARD

[C.O.]R.B. Reference: **MAX:355**

[You]r Reference:

45, BERKELEY STREET,
W.1.

Telegrams:
Avoncorb, London.

Telephone:
MAYFAIR 8400

12th March 1941.

Dear Mr. & Mrs. McGinty,

You will be interested
to know that we have received a
report from Australia about Patricia.
The report states that she has
settled do[wn] and her progress
is [describ]ed as very go... SHe is
in good health and is attending
the State School. I am afraid
this does not tell you anything
that you do not already know, but
you will be interested to have an
official report.

Yours truly,

Mr. & Mrs. A. J. McGinty,
50 Wyresdale Rd.,
Aintree,
Liverpool 9.

4316 Trista Court
Melbourne
Vic
Australia
25. 3. 4_

Dear Mr. McGinty

Pat is doing well in this grade. She is keen, very well behaved and is one of my monitors. She shows good ideas of controlling others. She seems very happy and contented and does not seem to be fretting in any way. She will go near the top of the grade when the final run for home. takes place. I shall send you a formal report at end of the half-year. Please accept all our good wishes and admiration for what you are taking I hope you will be able to give it back with compound interest. Yours faithfully

Thos. R. Clinnick M.B.

MD
CHILDREN'S OVERSEAS RECEPTION BOARD.

PLEASE NOTE CHANGE OF ADDRESS

DEVONSHIRE HOUSE,
45, BERKELEY STREET,
MAYFAIR PLACE, W.1.

Telegrams:
Avoncorb, London.

Telephone:
MAYFAIR 8866

C.O.R.B. Reference: MAX: 355

Your Reference:

18th March 1942.

Dear Mr. & Mrs. McGinty,

We have just received reports from Australia on all the children in Victoria, including Patricia. These were of course, written a month or two ago.

She is in very good health, and is happy and contented. She is making good progress in grade 4 at the State School, where she is popular with teachers and scholars. You will have heard she has been a class monitor.

Yours truly,

Elspeth Davies

Mr. & Mrs. A.J. McGinty.

The following was sent to parents in the light of rumours of a possible Japanese attack on Australia:

CHILDREN'S OVERSEAS RECEPTION BOARD.

Devonshire House,
Mayfair Place,
London, W.1.

20th March, 1942.

Dear *Mr. & Mrs. McGinty*

I know that parents whose children are in Australia, find it difficult not to feel some anxiety for them at this time.

I should like you to know that the Board is in close touch with its representative in Australia who reports that arrangements have been made by the Authorities to evacuate school children from danger points if this should at any time be considered necessary.

I am sure that parents can have complete confidence in the foster-parents and in the welfare authorities who have been looking after the children for the past 18 months. The welfare of the children is uppermost in their minds and from all reports we have received, parents can rely on any plans they make for the children's safety and welfare.

You may rest assured that should it be decided to evacuate children from any district the parents will be informed as soon as possible by the Board. In one or two instances private arrangements have already been made by individual foster-parents or schools, to move children inland, but there has as yet been no official evacuation.

If you are feeling anxious at any time, or worried by rumours or reports, I would ask you to remember that Mrs. Davies will certainly keep you informed of any developments affecting the children. They are in very good hands, and their foster-parents and the welfare authorities will always take every possible care of them.

Yours truly,

Marjorie Maxse

Director.

CHILDREN'S OVERSEAS RECEPTION BOARD,
Devonshire House,
Mayfair Place,
W.1.

28th October, 1942.

Dear Mr. & Mr. McGinly,

Mrs. Miles Davies, the head of the
Welfare Section of this office, who is
already well-known to you, will be in
Liverpool on Saturday, 7th November, and
I hope you will be able to attend a meeting
on that day at 3.30 p.m. at the Education
Offices, 14, St.Thomas Street, Liverpool 1,
when she will discuss various questions
affecting the children overseas, such as
education, training, employment and national
service, and supply general information.

Yours truly,

Marjorie Maxse

Director.

Please bring this letter with you.

THE BRITISH BROADCASTING CORPORATION

Broadcasting House, London, W. 1
Euston 3400
TELEPHONE: WELBECK 4468   TELEGRAMS: BROADCASTS, LONDON

Reference EP/EM   15th April 1943

Dear Mrs. McGinty

We were distressed to learn from your letter
received today that you have not yet had an
opportunity of recording a message to Patricia.
It happens that we hare holding a session
in public at the BBC Exhibition and I am
enclosing a formal letter of invitation.

Would you please let me know by return
if you can accept, as there will not be
another session from Manchester for some
time.

Yours sincerely,

Cuies Maxwell

for Director of Empire Programmes.

Mrs. McGinty
50 Wyresdale Road
Aintree
Liverpool. 9.

THE BRITISH BROADCASTING CORPORATION

Broadcasting House, London, W. 1

TELEPHONE: ~~WELBECK~~ Euston 3400. TELEGRAMS: BROADCASTS, LONDON

Reference: PP/EM   15th April 1943

Mr. and Mrs. McGinty
50 Wyresdale Road
Aintree, Liverpool 9.

Dear Mr. and Mrs. McGinty

We should be glad if you could come to The Art
Gallery, Mosely Street, Manchester   on 21st April
at 4 p.m.   to record a short message to your
child overseas.   It will be included in one of
the programmes "Hello Children" to be broadcast
in our Overseas Service within the next few
weeks.   The children concerned will be cabled
about time and wavelength.

If you are able to come the enclosed form must
be returned, completed, ~~within four days~~ to
Broadcasting House, London.   Your joint
message should last for thirty seconds only,
i.e. about 90 words.

The B.B.C. is willing to refund travelling
expenses in any cases where parents would
otherwise not be able to make the journey.

Yours faithfully,

Elsie Maxwell

for Director of Empire Programmes

Mr. and Mrs. McGinty.

CHILDREN'S OVERSEAS RECEPTION BOARD.
Devonshire House,
Mayfair Place,
LONDON, W.1.

28th July, 1943.

Dear Sir/Madam,

Free Cables.

At two meetings held recently at Devonshire House for parents in the London area, I was asked to approach the Cable and Wireless Company with a request that there should either be a change of messages or some additions to meet the needs of the growing children.

I got into touch with Cable and Wireless to see if such a suggestion would be practicable, and I am sorry to say that owing to the amount of labour involved both in this country and in the Dominions, and the material and printing of new cards, the Company very much regret that they cannot meet this request.

I feel that this is a not unreasonable attitude on the part of Cable and Wireless in view of the fact that for three years now they have undertaken the free transmission of cables to and from all C.O.R.B. children in the Dominions. I feel sure parents will understand this and be prepared to send any special cable which may be necessary at their own cost.

I took the opportunity of conveying to Cable and Wireless the grateful thanks expressed at the meeting.

Parcels.

Some parents have had difficulties recently because parcels posted in the ordinary way have been stopped by the Customs Authorities. Three customs declaration forms (C) and one despatch note should be completed for each parcel and sent to this Office. Two of the declaration forms and the despatch note will then be stamped and returned to you, so that one declaration form can be affixed to the parcel and the other two forms handed in with the parcel at the Post Office. There should then be no further difficulty.

Airgraph Letters.

Airgraph letters can now be sent to the children in Australia. The necessary form (price 8d.) can be obtained at any post office.

Transmission of Funds to Australia.

On several occasions questions have been asked about sending money to the children or foster-parents in Australia. This can be arranged through a bank or through the Post Office by means of an Imperial Money Order. Most banks are willing to assist in this way even if you have no account. Under a recent arrangement, the Postal Authorities in this country notify the Authorities overseas direct of sums being transmitted by Imperial Money Order, so that if one of your letters is lost in transit this does not mean that the money will not reach the payee.

Yours truly,

Marjorie Maxse

Director.

THE BRITISH BROADCASTING CORPORATION

Broadcasting House, London, W. 1

TELEPHONE: ~~EUSTON 3400~~   TELEGRAMS: BROADCASTS, LONDON

EUSTON 3400   BROADCASTS, TELEX, LONDON.

Reference: PP/EM

8th November 1943

Dear Mr. McGinty

Thank you for your letter of October 31st.

It is possible that Patricia has recorded a message
which has not yet been broadcast. Unfortunately,
owing to circuit conditions, we have not received
any 'Hello Patents' programmes from Australia
since May. We have asked the Australian
Broadcasting Commission to send us by air mail any
programmes which are already complete. When they
arrive we hope to broadcast them in the Home Service
but, if not, we shall certainly give parents an
opportunity of hearing their children's voices.

Should Patricia's message be among those sent
you will certainly be notified.

Yours sincerely

Elsie Maxwell.

for Assistant Controller (Overseas Services)

Arthur McGinty, Esq.
50 Wyresdale Road
Aintree
Liverpool 9

EM/EM

Children's Overseas Reception Board.

9 February 1944

Dear Sir/Madam,

Now that the tide of war is turning in our favour, I know that many parents who sent their children to the Dominions in 1940 under the CORB scheme are asking how soon after the war the children will return. I can fully understand and deeply sympathise with the feelings of parents who have been separated from their children for three and a half years. It is only natural that they should wish the separation to come to an end as soon as possible......

When hostilities in Europe are over, the CORB children will be able to return immediately shipping is available, and I hope that there will not be much delay. I am afraid however, that it will take longer to arrange for the passages of children in South Africa owing to the greater distance and to transport difficulties, while the return of children in Australia and New Zealand will depend upon conditions in the Pacific and Indian Oceans. To all parents I would say that there is no reason to worry , the Board will do its best to see that the children are brought home as soon as safe passages are assured and as soon as there are ships to carry them......'

In the same letter there is an indication that some children did not want to return for very valid reasons.

'.....The Board has asked parents not to bring their children back without their written consent, as in some cases their children have found good openings in the Dominions and wish to stay there or the parents themselves wish to go out and join their families. I can assure parents who fall into this category that they will be consulted in writing before any arrangements are made for their children to return. The Board has always foreseen the possibility that some of the children evacuated under its auspices would wish to take advantage of the opportunities open to them in the Dominions and that neither they nor their parents would wish them to return to the uncertain conditions which will, at any rate for a certain time, prevail in post-war Europe...'

Paul Emrys Evans

THE BRITISH BROADCASTING CORPORATION

Broadcasting House, London, W. I
Euston 3400
TELEPHONE: WELBECK 4468 CABLES: BROADCASTS, LONDON
INLAND TELEGRAMS: BROADCASTS, TELEX, LONDON

Reference 07/GO/EM   1st May 1944.

Dear Mr. McGinty,

Thank you for your letter. We cannot
issue the exact text of the messages
broadcast in the 'Hello Parents' programmes, but as your's is a special case
we shall do our best for you.   This is
roughly what Patricia said in the programme,
of 12th April:

"Hello Mum and Dad - this is your
daughter Pat saying hello from Melbourne.
How are Nin and Gran getting on - does Nin
still do the sword dance with the two
pokers ? How is Uncle Wal and Uncle Frank ?
Remember me to the Atkins, the Sheppherds
and Barbara and Kathleen and all my old
friends.   I'll be going to Preston High
School after Christmas to learn dressmaking.
I'm keeping in good health and am quite happy
here though I'd like to see you all again.
Aunty Marge has got a baby girl named
Carolyne and she is four months old. Cheerio
Mum - Dad and Nin.   I'll be seeing you all
soon - best wishes from all at Preson.
Lots of love from Pat."

Yours sincerely,

[signature]

for Assistant Controller (Overseas Services).

E. McGinty Esq.
50 Wyresdale Road
Aintree
Liverpool 9.

CHILDREN'S OVERSEAS RECEPTION BOARD,
Devonshire House,
Mayfair Place,
LONDON, W.1.

Tel.No.
MAYfair 8866.
Ref.No.

20th June, 1945.

Dear Sir/Madam,

You will be glad to know that arrangements are being made for
the children evacuated to Australia and New Zealand under the
Children's Overseas Reception Scheme to return to the United
Kingdom as soon as possible. They will travel in official parties
in the care of escorts, (except possibly in the case of a few of the
oldest boys and girls), but at the present time it is impossible
to indicate how soon this will be.

The passage accommodation available for civilians is limited
and there are many calls upon it; also as long as hostilities with
Japan continue, military requirements must come first. This makes
it difficult to estimate when passages will be available for
individual children. We are anxious, however, to make the most of
any opportunities which occur, and I shall be glad, therefore, if you
will complete the enclosed form and return it to this office at once,
so that arrangements could be completed without delay. The form A.C.75
which you signed last summer referred to preliminary plans only, and
this document is required before passages can be booked.

Although we cannot tell you yet when your child/children are
likely to sail for home, we shall be able to advise you about three
to four weeks before they are likely to arrive in the United Kingdom,
and, after that, you will be told where and when to meet them,
although it is unlikely that you would be able to go to the port of
arrival.

Yours faithfully,

E S Nicholas
Deputy Director.

A.C.108.

Children's Overseas Reception Board.

August 1944

'........I should also like to take this opportunity of making it clear to parents who wish their children to return that, except for those who have special permission to remain overseas to complete an apprenticeship or course of training, all such children will be expected to return with the official party. If parents or foster parents wish to make special arrangements, the children will have to be withdrawn from the Scheme and neither the Board nor the Dominion Authorities will be able to accept any responsibility for their care or return to the United Kingdom. As passenger accommodation is likely to be very restricted for some considerable time after the cessation of hostilities, parents cannot hope to visit or fetch their children unless the foster parents are willing to keep them for an indefinite period and they themselves are prepared to meet all the expense of the return journey.

Yours faithfully,

Marjorie Maxse.

Director.

Patricia returned to England from Australia on the 'Stirling Castle' in November 1945. She arrived in Southampton and then met her parents at Lime Street Station in Liverpool.

thanks

This letter is unusual as it is written by an ex-evacuee in February 1999 to the nephew of her war-time teacher who, with a colleague, looked after her during her evacuation. Not only is it a letter of thanks, but also an interesting description of her own and the teacher's experience.

'Dear Mr. C.

..A week before the last war broke out your Aunt, Miss Chaney, a Music and Drama teacher and her friend, Miss Frogett an Art teacher, were called back out of retirement. The Government policy was to release the younger teachers from their jobs to enable them to join the forces.

During the evacuation of 1939, your aunt and her friend were given the task of escorting many young girls between the ages of eight and eleven years of age first to Whitstable in Kent and then to Gilfach Goch in Wales. I was one of those evacuees and shall always be grateful for their loving tender care. Considering they were maiden ladies without children of their own they seemed to understand the emotional need of us home-sick young people and supported us to the best of their abilities. Not only did they inspire us with their teaching methods but they were also responsible for our welfare outside of school hours.

What I remember about them is that they were both Vegetarians, with short cropped hair, wore trilby hats, tweed skirts, twin sets, string of pearls and well trodden brogues.

The village people laughed about them behind their backs. It was very strange in those days for people to be vegetarians. We children were quite upset because our teachers had taken the place of our parents. We retaliated by disturbing the peace in the valley. In those days most people tried to make a contribution to the shortage of food by rearing their own poultry. Early evening, as it grew dark, the evacuees used to let the chickens and hens out of their coops. Many an owner could be seen chasing their poultry down the main street blaspheming in Welsh on the way.

In those days Vegetarians were issued with special ration books which allowed them an allocation of honey and cheese in place of meat. One winter I was very sick with yellow jaundice and your Aunt gave me her whole month's allowance of honey. I feel sure she saved my life as I had also just got over whooping cough as well and was therefore physically weak.....

These dear ladies taught us drama to keep us occupied. They produced two pantomimes The first year Cinderella and the second the Pied Piper of Hamelin. There was a great shortage of paper, crayons, theatre clothes, scenery, in fact there was a great shortage of everything.

Somehow these enterprising teachers created these successful shows and we evacuees played to full houses every night. This was the first time some of the locals had ever seen a Pantomime. The performances took place in the local Church Hall.....During the performance of the second

Pantomime, every child in the village attended. We could hear the German bombers flying over on their way to bomb Swansea. The adults were very anxious to send us home after the performance, in fact we were encouraged to run home. We found this very exciting. Within two hours of the hall being emptied a German bomber was trying to escape from a British Spitfire and dropped its bombs on the mountains, with the exception of one which flattened the Church Hall. It was the first and last bomb that dropped on the valley but the authorities decided that all the evacuees should leave the valley and go to Canada.

It was chaos again for us children and your Aunt and her friend tried to comfort us. More forms were sent home to our parents. Most of our lessons from then on were focussed on Canada and big ships.....A week before we were supposed to sail for Canada a ship was sunk...and some of us spent the rest of the war in Wales.

Many of the children drifted back home and your Aunt and her friend were sent back to Kent. We were desolate.......

A very grateful pupil.'

M.W. Totnes

conclusion

Post war generations in Britain have never yet, and hopefully never will, go through the mixed experiences of the Second World War evacuees. As the letters indicate, some had a great time, others were not so lucky. As I have stated before, it is impossible to generalise about evacuee experiences because reactions to it were dependant on the individual's previous life.

Hundreds of people have shared their memories with me and those in this book are just a sample.

There are two comments which sum up the effect of evacuation which I will conclude with. The first is from Jim Bartley. I first used this as an introduction in the book 'I'll take that one' and I always refer to it in lectures on this topic. However, I make no apologies for using it again because, in my opinion, it expresses the views of many evacuees.

> *'All the time I was evacuated I used to tell myself that one day the war would be over and I could go back home. After the war we were living in a different part of London and I made my way back to where I used to live. The whole area had been completely obliterated during the first few days of the Blitz and I was quite unable to find the spot where my house once stood. This happened more than fifty years ago. I have lived in many other places. I now have a grown-up family of my own and I am a grandfather. I now have a lovely house.....but somehow I'm still waiting to go home'.*

The second is written by Rose Fairbairn (nee Hayden) who was evacuated from West Ham to Bruton in Somerset.

In her account she relates how she and her fellow evacuee, Joyce, described their life in London to some of the boys in the village where they were evacuated.

> *'Joyce and I told them of our lives in London, our families and homes, the smoke and fog, it's small narrow streets and tiny houses. But there was also something that could never be put into words, something*

indefinable....whatever it was, within a few short months it would be blown away by German bombs (*) and only remembered by our generation.

I always remember an old Jewish gentleman once saying 'he was homesick for the dead' not for any person, but for something that was gone from our lives forever'.

[* Just after this she returned to London and was caught up in a bombing raid. Her stepmother was killed and she and her father seriously injured.]

However, even though she can recall these memories, she describes later in her letter that ...*'something was, and still is, missing from my life'.*

8th June, 1946

To-day, as we celebrate victory, I send this personal message to you and all other boys and girls at school. For you have shared in the hardships and dangers of a total war and you have shared no less in the triumph of the Allied Nations.

I know you will always feel proud to belong to a country which was capable of such supreme effort; proud, too, of parents and elder brothers and sisters who by their courage, endurance and enterprise brought victory. May these qualities be yours as you grow up and join in the common effort to establish among the nations of the world unity and peace.

George R.I.

Certificate presented to evacuated children

BIBLIOGRAPHY

Armstrong E. 'Growing Up and Ducking Down'. pub. Minerva Press 1997

Parsons M. 'I'll take that one!' Dispelling the Myths of Civilian Evacuation 1939-45. Beckett Karlson. 1998